Table Of Contents

Introduction

Have you ever wondered what makes nature, science, or even people so fascinating? In this book, you'll find quirky tidbits and jaw-dropping facts about our world, where even the strangest ideas make perfect sense once you dive in! From the animal kingdom's most unexpected heroes to the brilliant inventions that shaped history, this book is packed with surprises that will leave you curious, amused, and hungry to learn more. So, grab your thinking cap, buckle up, and let's explore some of the coolest facts you never knew!

The Human Body

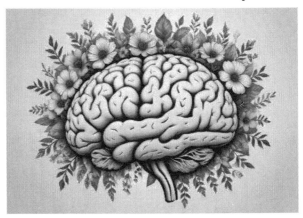

- Your brain contains about 86 billion neurons, which communicate through trillions of synapses, forming a complex network capable of processing vast amounts of information.

- Human bones are about five times stronger than steel of the same density, and ounce for ounce, stronger than concrete.

- If uncoiled, the DNA in all your cells would stretch from Earth to the sun and back over 600 times.

- The liver can regenerate itself even if as little as 25% remains, making it the only internal organ capable of substantial regeneration.

- The surface area of a human lung is roughly equal to that of a tennis court due to the tiny air sacs called alveoli.

- Your stomach lining replaces itself every 3-4 days to prevent the acidic environment from digesting the stomach itself.

- The acid in your stomach is so strong it can dissolve razor blades, though the mucous lining protects it from self-digestion.

- Humans shed about 50-100 strands of hair per day, yet still have around 100,000 strands on the scalp at any given time.

- An adult human is made up of about 7 octillion atoms, a number so vast it's nearly unimaginable.

- Your small intestine, despite its name, is about 18 feet long, making it longer than your entire height.

- The average person has about 4-6 liters of blood that circulates through the body 3 times per minute, meaning it travels over 12,000 miles each day.

- A single square inch of human skin has about 19 million cells and 60,000 melanocytes responsible for producing pigment.

- Your eyes can distinguish between around 10 million different colors, aided by the complex arrangement of rods and cones in the retina.

- The muscles that control your eyes are among the fastest-reacting muscles in your body, allowing them to adjust focus quickly.

- The fingerprints on each human are unique, and this is also true for your tongue print, which is another distinctive identifier.

- The brain consumes about 20% of your total energy, despite making up just 2% of your body weight.

- Your teeth are considered part of the skeletal system but do not regenerate after adult teeth emerge, unlike bones that can heal themselves.

- Blood vessels in an average adult, if laid end to end, would stretch over 60,000 miles, enough to circle the globe twice.

- The brain is capable of generating enough electrical power to light up a small LED bulb due to neural activity.

- Your body produces about 1-2 liters of saliva daily, essential for digestion and oral hygiene.

- The heart beats about 100,000 times a day, pumping nearly 2,000 gallons of blood through the circulatory system.

- The strongest muscle by weight in the human body is the masseter, or jaw muscle, which can apply up to 200 pounds of pressure on the molars.

- Your eyes can process images as quickly as 13 milliseconds, which is faster than a blink.

- The nose can identify over a trillion distinct scents due to the complex olfactory system, though not all are consciously recognized.

- Fingernails grow about four times faster than toenails, likely because of their increased exposure and use.

- Human saliva contains a natural painkiller called opiorphin, which is several times more powerful than morphine.

- The average lifespan of a taste bud is around 10 to 14 days, after which new ones replace them.

- There are about 650 skeletal muscles in the human body.

- Your bones are constantly being remodeled through a process called bone remodeling, where old bone is replaced by new.

- Each human foot has 26 bones, accounting for about one-quarter of the total bones in the body.

- The ears are responsible for balance, containing the vestibular system which helps maintain equilibrium.

- Goosebumps are a vestige of our evolutionary past when our hair would stand on end to make us appear larger and more intimidating.

- The brain can produce new neural pathways and adapt through a process known as neuroplasticity, even in adulthood.

- The average person breathes about 22,000 times a day, inhaling more than 2,600 gallons of air.

- The human embryo develops fingerprints within the first three months of gestation, which remain unique throughout life.

- Your liver performs over 500 essential functions, including detoxification, metabolism, and bile production.

- Your body has more bacterial cells than human cells, with over 100 trillion bacteria living mostly in your gut.

- The right lung is slightly larger than the left because the left lung needs space for the heart.

- Human teeth are nearly as hard as granite due to the high mineral content of enamel, the hardest substance in the body.

- Your body temperature varies throughout the day, typically lowest in the early morning and highest in the late afternoon.

- The average human can survive without food for several weeks but would only live a few days without water.

- The largest cell in the human body is the female egg, visible to the naked eye, while the smallest is the male sperm.

- The placenta, an organ that supports fetal development, is the only organ developed temporarily and then discarded after childbirth.

- Humans have a residual tailbone called the coccyx, a remnant of a vestigial tail.

- Your eyebrows help keep sweat and rain out of your eyes, serving as a protective barrier.

- Human muscles make up about 40% of total body weight, with the gluteus maximus (buttocks) being the largest.

- The pineal gland, located in the brain, is responsible for regulating sleep patterns by releasing melatonin.

- When a person blushes, the lining of the stomach also turns red due to increased blood flow.

- The knee joint is the largest joint in the body, critical for walking, running, and standing.

- Human skin completely replaces itself approximately every 27 days through a continuous process of shedding and regrowth.

- The cornea is the only part of the body with no blood supply; it gets oxygen directly through the air.

- Humans are capable of shedding around 30,000 to 40,000 dead skin cells every minute.

- Eyelashes have an average lifespan of about five months, while the eyelash growth cycle has three phases: growth, degradation, and resting.

- The longest recorded time between two twins being born is 87 days.

- The fastest growing nail is on your middle finger, while the slowest is on your thumb.

- During your lifetime, you will produce enough saliva to fill two swimming pools.

- A sneeze generates a wind of 100 mph and can send 100,000 germs into the air.

- Your brain uses 20% of the total oxygen and blood in your body.

- If you could unfold an adult's brain, it would be about the size of a pillowcase.

- Babies are born with 300 bones, but by adulthood, the number reduces to 206 due to the fusion of several bones.

- The smallest bone in the human body is the stapes bone located in the ear; it is smaller than a grain of rice.

- You breathe on average about 8,409,600 times a year.

- More than half of your bones are located in the hands, wrists, feet, and ankles.

- It takes 17 muscles to smile and 43 to frown.

- The human body contains about 0.2 milligrams of gold, most of which is in the blood.

- Human hair is virtually indestructible aside from its flammability — it decays so slowly that it is practically non-decomposable.

- The width of your armspan stretched out is approximately equal to your total height.

- The human body can detect taste in .0015 seconds, which is faster than the blink of an eye.

- Some people have an extra rib, known as a cervical rib, which can sometimes cause health issues like nerve compression.

- Human bones are hollow in structure but filled with bone marrow, a spongy tissue that produces around 500 billion blood cells daily.

The Animal Kingdom

- Octopuses have three hearts; two pump blood to the gills, while the third circulates blood to the body.

- Dolphins can recognize themselves in mirrors, demonstrating self-awareness similar to humans and great apes.

- Crows use tools like sticks and leaves to probe for insects and solve problems.

- Elephants are capable of empathy, helping each other out and showing emotional intelligence.

- Male lions rest for up to 20 hours a day, leaving most of the hunting to lionesses.

- Koalas sleep for up to 18 hours a day due to a low-calorie diet of eucalyptus leaves.

- Bats navigate in complete darkness using echolocation, emitting high-pitched sounds that bounce off objects.

- Humpback whales create complex "songs" lasting up to 20 minutes and traveling great distances underwater.

- Penguins can dive up to 1,500 feet and hold their breath for over 20 minutes while hunting.

- African elephants communicate through infrasound, allowing messages to travel miles.

- Gorillas live in family groups led by a dominant silverback male who protects the group.

- Octopuses squeeze through tiny openings since their bodies lack bones and are highly flexible.

- Parrots mimic human speech due to their highly developed syrinx, a vocal organ unique to birds.

- Male peacocks fan out colorful feathers to attract mates and intimidate rivals.

- Orcas hunt in coordinated groups, using strategies tailored to their prey.

- Horses can sleep standing up due to the stay apparatus, a mechanism in their legs.

- Rabbits are crepuscular, meaning they are most active during dawn and dusk.

- Tigers are solitary hunters with territories spanning hundreds of square miles.

- Kangaroos use muscular tails as a fifth limb to balance while hopping.

- Chimpanzees use sticks to fish for termites and leaves as sponges to soak up water.

- Sea lions recognize individual voices of their mates and offspring.

- Raccoons open jars, doors, and latches, demonstrating impressive problem-solving skills.

- Beavers build elaborate dams and lodges to create safe habitats, and their teeth never stop growing.

- Zebras have unique stripe patterns, like fingerprints, used for identification within herds.

- Great white sharks have rows of serrated teeth that are continuously replaced.

- Pigeons can find their way home from thousands of miles away due to magnetoreception.

- Bald eagles mate for life and build enormous nests they return to year after year.

- Clownfish form symbiotic relationships with sea anemones, gaining protection in exchange for nutrients.

- Sloths have specialized claws that help them hang from branches, descending only weekly to defecate.

- Snow leopards leap up to 50 feet to catch prey or cross rocky terrains.

- Cheetahs are the fastest land animals, reaching speeds up to 70 mph.

- Puffins hold multiple fish at once in their beaks, feeding efficiently.

- Coyotes thrive in urban environments, eating a wide variety of foods, including garbage.

- Hummingbirds have a high metabolism, consuming half their body weight in nectar daily.

- Gorillas build fresh nests every night, either on the ground or in trees.

- Owls can rotate their heads up to 270 degrees due to unique neck vertebrae.

- Emperor penguins withstand freezing temperatures and incubate eggs on their feet to keep them warm.

- Cows have four-chambered stomachs that allow them to digest tough plant material.

- An octopus changes color and texture to blend seamlessly into its surroundings.

- Rattlesnakes have heat-sensing pits that help them locate warm-blooded prey.

- Camels can drink up to 40 gallons of water and store fat in their humps for energy.

- Albatrosses have wingspans exceeding 11 feet and can fly long distances without flapping.

- Leopards are strong swimmers and often store prey in trees to protect it from scavengers.

- Narwhals live in the Arctic and have long, spiraling tusks that are actually elongated canine teeth.

- Prairie dogs dig burrows with chambers and entry points for shelter and protection.

- Black bears go without food for months during hibernation, living off their fat reserves.

- Gorillas have thick, muscular arms that help them climb and knuckle-walk.

- Sea turtles navigate using Earth's magnetic field to return to hatching grounds.

- Hippopotamuses secrete a natural "sunblock" protecting their skin from UV rays.

- Meerkats have a sentinel system, where one guards while others forage or play.

- Orangutans build nests high in trees using leaves and branches.

- Baleen whales filter-feed by gulping vast amounts of water and krill.

- Sea otters have thick fur and use rocks to crack open shellfish.

- Wolves can travel up to 30 miles a day to find food, marking their territory.

- Koalas eat eucalyptus leaves, which are toxic to most other animals.

- Female lions do most of the hunting while males guard the pride's territory.

- Crocodiles have strong jaws that exert thousands of pounds of pressure.

- Male peacocks molt their feathers annually, regrowing them for the next mating season.

- Honeybees perform a "waggle dance" to communicate food sources to hive mates.

- Bald eagles have powerful talons that snatch fish directly out of the water.

- Frogs have specialized skin that absorbs oxygen directly from water.

- The African grey parrot mimics human speech and has an impressive vocabulary.

- Prairie dogs have sophisticated calls conveying specific predator information.

- Horses have excellent peripheral vision due to eye positioning.

- Woodpeckers have long tongues that reach into crevices for insects.

- Seals slow down their heart rates to conserve oxygen while diving deep.

- Elephants communicate using low-frequency rumbles that travel long distances.

- Chimpanzees have opposable thumbs and toes for grasping branches.

- Red foxes adapt to diverse environments, from forests to cities.

- Male deer shed antlers annually and regrow them for mating season.

- Otters live in family groups and use vocalizations to coordinate hunting.

- Polar bears have blubber up to four inches thick to insulate from cold.

- Lemurs use vocalizations to coordinate group activities.

- Male emperor penguins incubate eggs through the Antarctic winter.

- Monkeys have prehensile tails used to grip branches and provide stability.

- Snow leopards have large nasal passages that warm the cold air.

- The gray wolf's howl is key for coordinating pack activities.

- Male orangutans develop cheek flaps that make them appear larger.

- Humpback whales migrate thousands of miles from feeding to breeding grounds.

- Coyotes have learned to coexist with humans, foraging in suburban areas.

- Hippos are among Africa's most dangerous animals, causing more human deaths than lions.

- Jaguars are powerful swimmers, often hunting prey in water.

- The Arctic fox's fur changes color to blend with summer or winter terrain.

- Platypuses sense electric fields using specialized receptors on their bills.

- Peregrine falcons are the fastest birds, diving at speeds over 200 mph.

- Great white sharks detect electromagnetic fields of prey using ampullae of Lorenzini.

- Giraffes have specialized valves in their neck arteries that prevent blood from rushing to the head when bending down.

- Elephants are the only mammals incapable of jumping due to their massive body weight and leg structure.

- Honey never spoils, and edible honey has been found in ancient Egyptian tombs over 3,000 years old.

- Sea otters hold hands while sleeping to prevent drifting apart in currents, known as "rafting."

- Male seahorses are the ones who carry and give birth to the offspring.

- Naked mole rats are nearly immune to cancer and can survive up to 18 minutes without oxygen.

- Penguins can drink seawater due to a special gland filtering excess salt from their bloodstream.

- The axolotl, a salamander, can regenerate limbs, spinal cords, and even parts of its brain.

- Male bowerbirds build elaborate structures to attract mates, often decorating them with colorful objects.

- Orcas use coordinated attacks to create waves that knock seals off ice floes.

- Vampire bats share blood meals with hungry roost-mates to ensure group survival.

- Flamingos get their pink coloring from the carotenoid pigments in algae and shrimp they eat.

- Narwhals, the "unicorns of the sea," have long, spiraling tusks that are elongated teeth.

- The mimic octopus can change its shape and behavior to impersonate other marine animals.

- Male praying mantises risk being eaten by females during mating, but well-fed females rarely kill males.

- Arctic ground squirrels can lower body temperature below freezing during hibernation.

- The common swift can stay airborne for up to 10 months, eating and sleeping in flight.

- Japanese macaques, or snow monkeys, bathe in hot springs and wash sweet potatoes in water.

- The immortal jellyfish reverts to its juvenile form after maturity, potentially living indefinitely.

- Sperm whales have the largest brains of any animal, weighing up to 17 pounds.

- Chameleons independently control their two eyes, looking in different directions simultaneously.

- The mantled howler monkey has an enlarged hyoid bone, enabling deafening roars heard miles away.

- Tasmanian devils produce a pungent odor when stressed and can devour entire carcasses, bones and all.

- Electric eels generate electric shocks up to 600 volts to stun prey or deter predators.

- The peregrine falcon is the fastest animal, reaching speeds over 240 mph during hunting dives.

- The blue-ringed octopus is highly venomous, with toxins strong enough to kill humans.

- African wild dogs have a unique social structure where all pack members care for the alpha pair's pups.

- The bearded vulture feeds mostly on bone marrow, obtained by dropping bones from heights.

- Leafcutter ants practice agriculture, cultivating fungi on harvested leaves.

- Snow leopards have long, thick tails that aid balance and provide warmth like a scarf.

- Male pufferfish create intricate sand circles to attract mates, which can take days.

- Meerkats have "sentry" members that keep watch for predators while others forage.

- Barn owls locate prey in complete darkness using asymmetrical ears to pinpoint sounds.

- Male frigatebirds inflate bright red throat pouches to attract females during the breeding season.

- The shoebill stork makes a unique bill-clattering sound heard from a distance.

- Male walruses produce bell-like underwater sounds during mating to attract females.

- Some ant species have "soldiers" with large heads that block nest entrances.

- African elephants recognize up to 100 different voices, distinguishing friend from foe.

- The hoatzin, or stinkbird, digests food through bacterial fermentation, resulting in a foul odor.

- Sea cucumbers can expel their internal organs to deter predators, later regenerating them.

- The Iberian ribbed newt can push its ribs through its skin as a defense mechanism.

- Prairie dogs have a complex language system, with specific calls for various predators.

- The pistol shrimp creates a shockwave by snapping its claw, stunning prey and reaching temperatures hotter than the sun's surface.

- The proboscis monkey's large nose attracts mates and amplifies vocalizations.

- The common cuckoo lays eggs in other birds' nests, tricking them into raising its chicks.

- Vampire squids can turn themselves inside out, exposing phosphorescent arm tips to deter predators.

- Tree kangaroos live in trees despite being related to land-dwelling kangaroos.

- The coconut crab can grow up to three feet across and climbs trees in search of coconuts.

- Arctic foxes change their fur color seasonally to blend with snow or summer terrain.

- The monarch butterfly migrates thousands of miles from Canada to Mexico over multiple generations.

- The mimic poison frog lays eggs in separate pools, transporting tadpoles on its back.

- The thylacine, or Tasmanian tiger, was the largest known carnivorous marsupial before extinction.

Crazy Beliefs of the Past

- In medieval Europe, animals were sometimes put on trial for crimes like murder or property destruction.

- Phrenology was the belief that the shape and bumps of one's skull could determine personality traits and intelligence.

- The miasma theory claimed diseases like cholera and the plague were caused by "bad air" or "miasmas" rather than by germs.

- Alchemists aimed to transmute base metals into gold and discover the elixir of life, blending early chemistry with mysticism.

- Flat Earth theory posited that the Earth was a flat disc, a widely accepted belief before the Greeks proposed it was round.

- Bloodletting was a medical practice that drained blood to cure illnesses, believed to rebalance bodily humors, but often harmful.

- The divine right of kings held that monarchs ruled directly by God's authority and were accountable only to divine judgment.

- Humorism proposed that health depended on balancing four humors: blood, phlegm, yellow bile, and black bile.

- Alchemists believed all matter was composed of four elements: earth, air, fire, and water.

- Mercury was once used as a treatment for ailments like syphilis, though it often led to severe mercury poisoning.

- The Salem witch trials led to mass hysteria and execution of suspected witches based on dubious evidence.

- Some ancient tribes believed that eating their enemies could transfer their strength and courage.

- Mandrake roots were believed to scream and kill anyone who heard them when pulled from the ground.

- Explorers believed in mythical sea monsters like the Kraken or Leviathan that could sink ships.

- Spontaneous generation proposed that living organisms could arise directly from non-living matter.

- The lunar lunacy effect claimed that the moon's phases made people insane, leading to the term "lunatic."

- Necromancy involved summoning the dead or communicating with spirits to predict the future.

- Human sacrifice was believed to appease gods and ensure good harvests or victories in ancient cultures.

- Ground-up animal parts, like rhino horn or viper flesh, were used as remedies for various ailments.

- Alchemists searched for the elixir of immortality, believed to grant eternal life and health.

- The king's touch was thought to cure diseases like scrofula.

- Exorcism sought to treat mental illness by casting out demons rather than using medical care.

- The curse of Tutankhamun was blamed for the deaths of explorers who opened King Tut's tomb.

- Medieval explorers believed in Prester John, a mythical Christian king with a vast kingdom in Asia or Africa.

- Theosophists believed that humanity originated from Venus and was guided by ascended masters.

- The wandering womb theory blamed a displaced uterus for hysteria and other ailments in women.

- Lobotomies were used to treat mental illness but often caused severe impairments.

- European folklore included lycanthropy, the ability of humans to transform into wolves.

- Alchemists believed they could grow a tiny human called a homunculus in a jar.

- Draining marshes was thought to cure diseases like malaria due to its association with stagnant water.

Bizarre Traditions and Customs

- The "Monkey Buffet Festival" in Thailand provides a feast for thousands of monkeys, who are revered as symbols of prosperity and luck.

- The "baby jumping" festival in Spain, known as El Colacho, involves men dressed as devils leaping over rows of babies to cleanse them of sin and ward off evil spirits.

- In the Satere-Mawe tribe in the Amazon, boys undergo a coming-of-age ritual where they must wear gloves filled with bullet ants, which have the world's most painful sting.

- In India, people celebrate the "Holi" festival by throwing vibrant colored powders and water at each other to mark the victory of good over evil and the arrival of spring.

- The Japanese tradition of "Namahage" involves men dressed as ogres visiting homes on New Year's Eve to scare children into being obedient in the coming year.

- During the Day of the Dead (Dia de los Muertos) in Mexico, families build altars, decorate graves, and hold celebrations to honor their deceased loved ones.

- In Denmark, people throw plates and cups at their friends' doors on New Year's Eve, believing that the bigger the pile, the more friends one will have in the coming year.

- In the Fulani tribe of West Africa, young men endure the "Sharo" ritual, a test of bravery where they are flogged with whips in a public display.

- The Japanese custom of "Otoshi-dama" involves adults giving children money in decorated envelopes to celebrate the New Year.

- In Greece, people wear amulets called "mati," or evil eye charms, to protect themselves from the envious looks that can cause bad luck.

- In the U.K., people celebrate "Guy Fawkes Night" with fireworks and bonfires to commemorate the failure of the Gunpowder Plot of 1605.

- In Papua New Guinea, the Dani people traditionally preserved their ancestors by smoking the bodies and displaying them in their villages.

- The "Kanamara Matsuri" in Japan, or Festival of the Steel Phallus, celebrates fertility, good health, and safe childbirth with parades and phallic-shaped objects.

- The Spanish festival "La Tomatina" involves tens of thousands of participants throwing tomatoes at each other in a giant food fight.

- In Indonesia, the Toraja people dig up their deceased relatives every few years, clean their remains, and dress them in new clothes as a sign of respect.

- The Ivrea Carnival in Italy features the Battle of the Oranges, where participants throw oranges at each other to reenact an ancient revolt.

- In South Korea, the "Boknal" tradition involves eating a hot bowl of chicken soup on the hottest days to cool down and boost stamina.

- In Germany, when single men and women reach their 30th birthday, they often have to sweep steps or clean public spaces to earn kisses from friends.

- The "Thaipusam" festival in Malaysia and Singapore sees devotees piercing their bodies with hooks and skewers while carrying elaborate structures called "kavadis."

- During "La Pourcailhade" in France, participants compete in pig-related events like piglet racing and sausage eating.

- In India, the "Banni" festival involves men fighting each other with sticks to appease the deity Mala-Malleshwara and earn blessings.

- In the U.K., "Cheese Rolling" is an annual competition where people chase a rolling wheel of cheese down a steep hill.

- The "Up-Helly-Aa" festival in Scotland celebrates Viking heritage with torchlight processions and the ceremonial burning of a longship.

- The Japanese practice of "Hikikomori" involves people isolating themselves from society for months or even years, often due to social anxiety.

- In Bolivia, people build shrines and make offerings to "Ekeko," a god of abundance, by giving him miniature versions of things they desire.

- The Tibetan sky burial involves placing the deceased on a mountaintop to be consumed by vultures, believed to be an act of compassion and charity.

- In the Philippines, penitents re-enact the crucifixion of Jesus on Good Friday, with some even allowing themselves to be nailed to crosses.

- In the U.S., "Groundhog Day" determines the arrival of spring based on whether a groundhog sees its shadow.

- In the "Baby Tossing" ceremony in India, infants are thrown from a temple roof to be caught by people holding a cloth below as a good luck ritual.

- In Finland, wife-carrying competitions see men racing while carrying their partners over obstacle courses, with the prize often being the wife's weight in beer.

- In Peru, the annual "Takanakuy" festival involves people settling disputes by fist-fighting each other in public before reconciling with a drink.

- In South Africa, some people celebrate New Year's Eve by throwing old furniture out of windows to symbolize letting go of the past.

- In the Czech Republic, unmarried women throw shoes over their shoulders on Christmas Eve to predict if they'll marry in the coming year.

- The "Mud Festival" in South Korea involves people bathing, wrestling, and sliding in mud for fun and to promote skincare benefits.

- In Romania, the "Bear Dance" sees people dressing as bears and dancing to ward off evil spirits and bring good luck for the New Year.

- In Spain, people eat 12 grapes at midnight on New Year's Eve to ensure good fortune in each month of the coming year.

- In Japan, people visit temples to ring bells 108 times on New Year's Eve to symbolize purging worldly desires and starting the new year fresh.

- In the U.K., people celebrate "May Day" by dancing around a maypole and crowning a May Queen to welcome the spring season.

- In Denmark, students celebrate high school graduation by driving around in decorated trucks, honking horns, and stopping at friends' houses to party.

- In Austria, people dress as Krampus, a mythical creature that accompanies Saint Nicholas, to scare misbehaving children into behaving better.

Our Beloved Pets

- 66% of U.S. households, equivalent to 86.9 million homes, own a pet.

- Dogs are the most popular pet in the U.S. 65.1 million U.S. households own a dog. Cats are the second most popular, owned by 46.5 million households, followed by freshwater fish (11.1 million).

- Dogs have about 300 million olfactory receptors in their noses, compared to humans who only have 6 million, making their sense of smell incredibly sensitive.

- Cats have a specialized collarbone that allows them to always land on their feet when falling from a height, known as the "righting reflex."

- Dogs communicate with humans through a range of facial expressions, using their eyebrows to show sadness or happiness.

- Cats can rotate their ears 180 degrees to pinpoint sounds, helping them detect prey and distinguish between different noises.

- Some cats are allergic to humans. Just like humans, animals can have allergies to a variety of substances, and although it's rare, some pets are allergic to our dead skin cells, known as dander.

- Dogs can recognize human emotions through their sense of smell, reacting differently to the scent of sweat produced from stress versus exercise.

- Cats knead with their paws, a behavior that originates from kittenhood when they knead their mother's belly to stimulate milk flow.

- Dogs can be trained to detect health conditions like diabetes or seizures by sensing changes in a person's breath or sweat.

- Cats use "slow blinking" to communicate affection, mimicking the way they blink at their owners when they feel safe.

- Over half of pet owners (51%) view their pets as family members equal to humans.

- Dogs and cats have whiskers with specialized nerve endings, which help them gauge distances, detect movement, and navigate in the dark.

- Dogs are capable of learning and remembering over 200 words and commands, similar to the language ability of a 2-year-old human child.

- Cats have retractable claws to keep them sharp and ready for hunting, which also prevents wear and tear from everyday activities.

- 42% of dog owners and 43% of cat owners acquired their pets from a store, while 38% of dog owners and 40% of cat owners adopted from shelters.

- Dogs dream like humans, often exhibiting twitching, barking, or paddling movements while asleep, indicating active dreaming.

- Dogs wag their tails in different directions based on their emotions, with a rightward wag indicating happiness and a leftward wag indicating anxiety.

- Cats can recognize their owner's voice but often choose to ignore commands, showing that they understand more than they respond to.

- Dogs produce oxytocin, the "love hormone," when they interact with their owners, similar to how humans feel affection.

- Essential expenses for dogs cost an average of $1,533 annually, including boarding, veterinary care, and pet insurance.

- Cats use grooming as a way to bond with their owners and other cats, a behavior called allogrooming that reduces stress.

- Dogs have a strong pack mentality and can experience separation anxiety when left alone, sometimes resulting in destructive behavior.

- Dogs are the most popular pet in the U.S., with 65.1 million households owning a dog.

- Cats have a unique purring frequency that is believed to promote healing and reduce stress, both in themselves and their owners.

- Dogs are capable of mimicking their owner's emotions through a phenomenon known as emotional contagion.

- Cats' purrs can help reduce anxiety and blood pressure in humans, making them therapeutic companions.

- Dogs prefer routine and often develop behaviors based on their daily schedule, like anticipating feeding time or walks.

- Cats have a "hunting instinct" that persists even in domesticated cats, which is why they often bring gifts like birds or mice to their owners.

- Dogs can hear higher-pitched sounds than humans, detecting frequencies up to 65,000 Hz compared to our 20,000 Hz limit.

- Cats mark their territory by rubbing their heads against objects, transferring scent from glands located around their face.

- Dogs understand pointing gestures and follow them to find hidden treats or objects, a skill rarely found in non-primates.

- Cats can tolerate heat better than dogs, as they have sweat glands only in their paw pads and rely on licking to cool down.

- Dogs have a "smell print" as unique as a human fingerprint, and they use scent to identify each other and their human family members.

- Cats have a special meow that they use exclusively with humans, differing from the vocalizations used with other cats.

- Dogs evolved a specific facial muscle that allows them to raise their eyebrows, which makes them appear more expressive and appealing to humans.

- Cats' whiskers can detect even the slightest changes in airflow, helping them hunt or detect obstacles in the dark.

- 35% of Americans have more than one pet.

- Dogs show submission to humans and other dogs by rolling over and exposing their bellies, inviting friendly interaction.

- Cats have a specialized vision system that allows them to see in near darkness and detect motion more effectively than humans.

- Dogs tilt their heads to the side when listening to their owners because it helps them better locate and understand the sound source.

- Cats' grooming habits can reduce their owner's allergies, as their saliva contains an enzyme that breaks down allergens.

- Millennials make up the largest share of pet owners at 33%, followed by Gen X at 25% and baby boomers at 24%.

- Dogs interpret human body language and can learn to respond to subtle gestures or changes in posture.

- Cats have flexible spines and shoulder blades that allow them to squeeze through tight spaces and make high jumps.

- Dogs are capable of feeling jealousy, as studies show they become agitated when their owners show attention to other animals.

- Cats communicate their feelings through tail position, with a high, upright tail indicating confidence or friendliness.

- Dogs are capable of recognizing themselves in mirrors, an indication of self-awareness similar to humans and great apes.

- Cats are more likely to purr when they are happy or comfortable, using the sound as a means of communication.

- The percentage of households owning pets has increased from 56% in 1988 to 66% today.

- Dogs have a remarkable sense of direction and can often find their way back home even from long distances.

- Cats often sleep in a curled position, which helps conserve body heat and protect their vital organs while resting.

- Dogs rely on eye contact and facial cues to determine human emotions, adjusting their behavior accordingly.

- Cats use a "chirping" vocalization to mimic the calls of birds, often heard when they are watching birds from windows.

- Dogs have sweat glands on their paw pads and rely on panting to cool down their bodies during hot weather.

- Cats prefer high places, as it gives them a sense of security and an excellent vantage point for observing their surroundings.

- Dogs instinctively turn in circles before lying down, a behavior that may stem from ancestral wolves making nests in tall grass.

- Cats have a specialized layer behind their retinas called the tapetum lucidum, which reflects light and enhances night vision.

- Dogs are capable of empathy and can comfort humans who are crying or distressed, often seeking physical contact to soothe them.

- Cats can sense changes in weather through their heightened sense of smell and hearing, often seeking shelter before storms.

- Dogs are more sociable and thrive on interaction, often developing behaviors based on positive reinforcement from their owners.

- Cats use a distinctive "trilling" sound to communicate playfulness or affection, often directed at their owners.

- Dogs can detect earthquakes or natural disasters through their keen senses, sometimes exhibiting unusual behavior before the event.

- Cats' grooming habits help distribute natural oils across their fur, keeping it clean and shiny.

- Dogs can recognize family members after long absences and often react joyfully to their return.

- Cats may exhibit kneading behavior when resting on their owner's lap, a sign of comfort and security.

- Dogs have a heightened sensitivity to changes in the environment, alerting their owners to intruders or unusual occurrences.

- Cats have retractable claws that protect their sharpness while providing an advantage when hunting.

- Dogs have individual preferences for food and activities based on their breed, training, and upbringing.

- Cats often greet their owners with head bunting, a way to mark them with their scent and show affection.

- Dogs can understand tone and often react more to the pitch of a voice than the specific words spoken.

- Cats may over-groom when stressed or anxious, leading to bald patches or skin irritation.

- Gen Z pet owners are likelier to spoil their pets with birthday cakes (34%) and costumes (32%).

- Dogs can distinguish between identical twins using only their sense of smell.

- Cats have extra-sensitive hearing and can detect ultrasonic frequencies emitted by rodents and other small prey.

- Dogs can follow the direction of human pointing even as puppies, indicating a natural inclination to understand humans.

- Cats rely on their owner's habits to create a routine, often adjusting their own behaviors to align with feeding or play times.

- Dogs often "smile" by pulling back their lips to communicate friendliness or playfulness.

- Cats prefer horizontal or vertical scratching posts, which allow them to stretch their muscles while marking territory.

- Dogs can recognize their owner's vehicles from a distance by listening for the engine sound and smell.

- Cats may engage in "overgrooming" as a coping mechanism for anxiety or boredom.

- Dogs are capable of detecting human illnesses like cancer by picking up subtle changes in body odor.

- Cats can drink seawater due to their highly efficient kidneys, which filter out excess salt.

- Dogs are more responsive to hand signals than verbal commands due to their ability to understand non-verbal cues.

- Cats prefer drinking running water over stagnant, which is why they often drink from faucets.

- Dogs are more likely to trust people who smile, as they associate smiling faces with positive intentions.

- Cats have unique hunting instincts, often "playing" with prey to practice their skills.

- Dogs can develop a sense of time and often anticipate their owner's return home based on regular routines.

- Cats are highly territorial and may react aggressively to new animals entering their perceived space.

- Dogs often greet their owners by sniffing their faces and hands, using smell to gather information.

- Cats may communicate affection by nibbling on their owner's fingers or clothing, mimicking kitten behavior.

- Dogs prefer praise and food as rewards for training but may also respond well to toys or playtime.

- Cats instinctively hide signs of illness to protect themselves from predators, which can make diagnosing ailments challenging.

- Dogs can pick up on human social cues and will often mimic their owner's behavior or emotional state.

- Cats can differentiate between familiar and unfamiliar voices, often reacting only to their owner's calls.

- Dogs are more likely to follow eye contact when their owner is speaking directly to them.

- Cats may exhibit clinginess if they have formed a strong bond with their owner or feel threatened.

- Dogs prefer familiar routes during walks, which help them feel secure and minimize anxiety.

- Cats can differentiate between human expressions and will often mirror positive emotions like smiling.

- Dogs often show joy by wagging their tails and jumping, especially when reunited with their owners.

- Cats exhibit playful aggression during games, often grabbing and biting at toys as practice for hunting.

- Dogs may try to herd small children or animals due to their innate herding instincts.

- Cats are more active at night due to their crepuscular nature and may seek playtime or attention in the early morning.

- Dogs have an excellent memory for places and can often recall locations where they found food or toys.

- Cats often create bonds with other pets in the household and may groom or sleep near them.

- Dogs will often lean against their owners to seek comfort and show affection.

- Cats may imitate their owner's behavior or routine as a sign of bonding or seeking attention.

- Dogs use scent to mark their territory and will often return to the same spots to reinforce the mark.

- Cats often find comfort in small, enclosed spaces like boxes or bags, which mimic the security of a den.

- Dogs may sleep near their owner's bedroom or door to protect them and feel secure.

- Higher-income households are more likely to own pets, with 63% of those earning over $100,000 owning dogs.

Strange World Records and Abilities

- The longest recorded time someone voluntarily held their breath underwater is over 24 minutes.

- The longest recorded fingernails reached a combined length of over 28 feet.

- The shortest adult ever recorded stood at just 21.5 inches tall.

- The tallest adult ever recorded was 8 feet 11 inches tall.

- The heaviest person on record weighed over 1,400 pounds.

- The longest continuous period of time spent awake is 11 days.

- The fastest marathon time by a human running backward is 3 hours and 43 minutes.

- The fastest marathon time while juggling three balls, or "joggling," is 2 hours and 50 minutes.

- A woman once completed a marathon while pushing a triple stroller carrying her three children.

- The most tattoos a person has on their body is over 95% of their body covered.

- The most spoons balanced on a person's body at once is over 70.

- The world's longest hair on a living person measures over 18 feet.

- The longest mustache recorded measures over 14 feet.

- The oldest documented mother gave birth at the age of 74.

- The youngest recorded mother gave birth at age 5.

- The fastest recorded typing speed was over 200 words per minute.

- The world's longest time spent in a plank position is over 8 hours.

- The longest uninterrupted game of Monopoly lasted over 70 days.

- The fastest time for solving a Rubik's cube blindfolded is under 15 seconds.

- The fastest time for solving a 1000-piece jigsaw puzzle is under 2 hours.

- The longest time spent playing chess without a break is over 50 hours.

- The longest time spent in an ice bath is over 2 hours.

- The fastest person to drink a liter of beer completed the task in less than 2 seconds.

- The fastest person to eat 100 meters of spaghetti with their mouth is under 30 seconds.

- The most push-ups completed in 24 hours is over 46,000.

- The longest dance marathon lasted over 126 hours.

- The longest continuous time swinging on a swing set is over 32 hours.

- The most consecutive somersaults performed in a row is over 9,000.

- The longest single handshake lasted more than 33 hours.

- The longest time spinning a basketball on one finger is over 11 minutes.

- The fastest speed skiing backward is over 60 mph.

- The most hula hoops spun simultaneously is over 200.

- The longest time spent balancing on a tightrope is over 217 hours.

- The most consecutive backflips completed on a trampoline is over 3,000.

- The most tattooed woman has over 96% of her body covered in ink.

- The longest time someone has stayed on a surfboard is over 40 hours.

- The most tattoos given in 24 hours is over 800.

- The longest time someone has held a headstand is over 3 hours.

- The longest time spent balancing a book on one's head is over 6 hours.

- The longest distance someone has walked backward is over 13,000 kilometers.

- The longest distance cycled in a year is over 75,000 miles.

- The most marshmallows caught in one's mouth is over 75.

- The most boiled eggs eaten in one sitting is over 65.

- The fastest one-handed climb of Mount Everest is just over 6 hours.

- The most people crammed into a phone booth is over 25.

- The largest gathering of twins is over 6,000 pairs.

- The most jumps on a pogo stick in 24 hours is over 88,000.

- The longest hair ever grown on a man is over 26 feet.

- The fastest 100-meter sprint on stilts is under 15 seconds.

- The most ice cream scoops balanced on one cone is over 120.

- The largest number of balloons blown up in an hour is over 400.

- The longest human chain holding hands stretched over 1,000 miles.

- The longest interval between twin births is 87 days.

- The most watermelons cut on someone's stomach in a minute is over 40.

- The fastest time to complete a mile while skipping is under 10 minutes.

- The largest number of push-ups done by a dog is over 60 in a minute.

- The longest amount of time spent spinning plates on poles is over 6 hours.

- The longest time spent surfing a single wave is over 3 hours.

- The most people lying on beds of nails simultaneously is over 200.

- The largest underwater wedding involved over 300 divers.

- The longest time someone has held a bridge pose is over 3 hours.

- The fastest 100-meter sprint while wearing swim fins is under 15 seconds.

- The longest domino chain made from mattresses is over 1,000.

- The longest journey on a skateboard lasted over 7,500 miles.

- The longest beard ever measured was over 17 feet.

- The most high-fives given in a single minute is over 300.

- The fastest 100-meter sprint on all fours is under 17 seconds.

- The longest single handstand walk is over 1 mile.

- The longest string of continuous bubbles blown by a person is over 15 miles.

- The most wet sponges thrown at a face in one minute is over 60.

- The most juggling catches in one minute is over 500.

- The fastest time to eat a hot dog is under 10 seconds.

- The most balloons burst with one's teeth in a minute is over 20.

- The longest continuous skipping rope session lasted over 30 hours.

- The longest continuous ride on a Ferris wheel lasted over 50 hours.

- The largest collection of rubber ducks contains over 9,000 ducks.

- The fastest sprint while carrying a refrigerator is under 30 seconds.

- The largest collection of comic books is over 100,000 issues.

- The most straws stuffed into someone's mouth at once is over 400.

- The most snails on a person's face at one time is over 50.

- The most dice balanced on the edge of a playing card is over 200.

- The largest number of people playing hopscotch simultaneously is over 1,000.

- The longest time spent juggling five soccer balls is over 10 minutes.

- The most pizzas made in one hour is over 200.

- The most hamburgers made in one hour is over 500.

- The longest amount of time spent balancing a soccer ball on one's head is over 8 hours.

- The most people spooning simultaneously is over 1,000.

- The most T-shirts worn at once is over 250.

- The longest time spent lying in a bed of ice is over 3 hours.

- The fastest person to eat a bowl of pasta used only their mouth, finishing in less than 30 seconds.

- The longest leap from one building to another was a distance of over 30 feet.

- The most pencils balanced on one's face at once is over 20.

- The most times one person has circumnavigated the globe by plane is over 500.

- The largest number of people flossing simultaneously is over 20,000.

- The most darts thrown at a dartboard in one hour is over 500.

- The longest time spent paddling a canoe continuously is over 24 hours.

- The longest duration hula hooping underwater is over 3 minutes.

- The largest collection of rubber bands contains over 1 million bands.

- The fastest person to eat a 12-inch pizza did it in under 40 seconds.

- The fastest person to solve 10 chess puzzles consecutively did it in under 5 minutes.

- The longest time spent playing a single video game is over 40 hours.

- The most coins balanced on a single coin is over 60.

All about Dinosaurs

- Dinosaurs ruled the Earth for more than 160 million years, from the Triassic to the end of the Cretaceous period.

- The largest known dinosaur, Argentinosaurus, could reach lengths of up to 100 feet and weigh over 100 tons.

- Some dinosaurs, like Velociraptor, had feathers, suggesting a close evolutionary relationship with birds.

- The first dinosaur fossil was formally described in the early 19th century, giving rise to the field of paleontology.

- The T. rex had a bite force of over 12,000 pounds, one of the strongest bites ever known.

- Some herbivorous dinosaurs, such as Diplodocus, swallowed stones (gastroliths) to help grind food in their digestive system.

- Spinosaurus is believed to have been semi-aquatic, hunting for fish and spending significant time in the water.

- The Triassic-Jurassic extinction event wiped out around 50% of Earth's species, paving the way for dinosaurs to dominate the land.

- Stegosaurus had distinctive plates along its back, which may have been used for display or temperature regulation.

- The largest known carnivorous dinosaur, Giganotosaurus, was even bigger than T. rex.

- Some ankylosaurs had club-like tails, which they likely used for defense against predators.

- The horned dinosaur Triceratops had three facial horns and a bony frill that protected its neck.

- The fossilized bones of many dinosaurs reveal evidence of diseases like arthritis and bone infections.

- Some dinosaurs, like Iguanodon, had specialized thumb spikes that were likely used for defense.

- Pterosaurs, while often associated with dinosaurs, were actually flying reptiles that coexisted with them.

- The Archaeopteryx is considered a transitional species between non-avian dinosaurs and modern birds.

- The fossilized nests of some dinosaurs, such as Maiasaura, provide evidence of parental care.

- The first feathered dinosaur fossil, Sinosauropteryx, was discovered in China in the 1990s.

- Some dinosaurs, like Allosaurus, had serrated teeth to slice through the flesh of their prey.

- Fossilized dinosaur footprints are known as "ichnites," which can reveal behavior patterns like walking speeds and herding.

- The skull of Pachycephalosaurus was up to 10 inches thick, possibly used for head-butting contests.

- Sauropods, such as Apatosaurus, had long necks that helped them reach leaves high in trees.

- Fossilized dinosaur eggs have been found on every continent except Antarctica.

- Therizinosaurus had enormous claws up to 3 feet long, possibly for stripping leaves from branches.

- Some dinosaurs, like Brachiosaurus, had longer front legs than hind legs, allowing them to stand more upright.

- The mass extinction that wiped out the dinosaurs 66 million years ago was caused by a combination of volcanic activity and an asteroid impact.

- The Psittacosaurus had bristle-like structures on its tail that may have been used for display.

- The smallest known dinosaur, Microraptor, was about the size of a crow and had feathers on all four limbs.

- Hadrosaurs, like Parasaurolophus, are known for their distinctive crest, which may have amplified their calls.

- Fossilized amber containing prehistoric insects provides insight into the ecosystem of the dinosaurs' era.

- Carnotaurus had tiny arms, even smaller than those of T. rex, but had strong hind legs for running.

- Oviraptor fossils were once thought to be egg thieves because they were found near nests, but evidence shows they were likely caring for their own eggs.

- Some dinosaur bones have been found with preserved soft tissues, providing a glimpse into their biology.

- The long-necked dinosaur Diplodocus could whip its tail at high speeds, possibly as a defensive mechanism.

- Troodon had one of the largest brains relative to body size among dinosaurs, suggesting high intelligence.

- The name "dinosaur" means "terrible lizard" and was coined by Sir Richard Owen in the 1840s.

- Ankylosaurus had armored plates covering its back and a clubbed tail that could break bones.

- Ceratosaurus had distinctive horns above its eyes and on its snout, giving it a fearsome appearance.

- Fossil evidence suggests that some dinosaurs lived in polar regions during periods when the climate was warmer.

- Megalodon, often associated with dinosaurs, was actually a giant shark that lived millions of years after the dinosaurs.

- The sauropod Brontosaurus was once considered a misidentified Apatosaurus, but new research reinstated it as a distinct genus.

- Some dinosaurs likely migrated long distances, following seasonal changes in food availability.

- The fossilized remains of prehistoric plants show evidence of dinosaurs feeding on them.

- Diplodocus had a relatively small head compared to its enormous body, with peg-like teeth for stripping leaves.

- Velociraptors were smaller than depicted in movies, about the size of a turkey, and likely hunted in packs.

- Titanosaurs were among the last surviving sauropods and lived during the Late Cretaceous period.

- Fossilized footprints in China show evidence of herding behavior among sauropods.

- Deinonychus had a large, sickle-shaped claw on each foot that was likely used to slash at prey.

- The ceratopsid Styracosaurus had a frill adorned with long spikes, giving it a menacing appearance.

- The fossils of feathered dinosaurs like Caudipteryx support the theory that birds evolved from theropods.

Amazing Food Facts

- Potatoes were the first vegetable grown in space, planted by NASA and the University of Wisconsin. They were planted at the ISS (International Space Station).

- Chocolate was once used as currency by the ancient Aztecs and considered more valuable than gold.

- The color of a bell pepper can indicate its ripeness: green is unripe, yellow/orange is semi-ripe, and red is fully ripe.

- Cashews grow on the bottom of a cashew apple and are technically seeds rather than nuts.

- Pineapples can take up to two years to grow from planting to harvesting.

- The world's most expensive coffee, Kopi Luwak, is made using beans that have been eaten and excreted by civet cats.

- Nutmeg, when consumed in large amounts, can cause hallucinations due to its psychoactive compounds.

- Apples float in water because they are 25% air, which makes them buoyant.

- Bananas are technically berries, while strawberries are not classified as true berries.

- Tomatoes were once believed to be poisonous in Europe and called "wolf peaches."

- The pistachio is known as the "smiling nut" in Iran and the "happy nut" in China due to its partially open shell.

- The durian fruit, known for its strong odor, is banned from many public spaces in Southeast Asia.

- Saffron, made from the stigma of crocus flowers, is the world's most expensive spice by weight.

- Carrots were originally purple before being selectively bred for their orange color in the 17th century.

- Coconut water can be used as an emergency intravenous hydration fluid due to its electrolyte composition.

- An egg will sink in fresh water but can float in salt water because adding salt increases the water's density, making it higher than that of the egg.

- Worcestershire sauce contains anchovies that have been fermented for up to two years before bottling.

- The world's largest food fight, La Tomatina, takes place annually in Spain, involving thousands of participants throwing tomatoes.

- The origin of the sandwich is attributed to John Montagu, the 4th Earl of Sandwich, who wanted a meal he could eat without leaving the gaming table.

- The world's most expensive cheese, Pule, is made from Balkan donkey milk and costs over $1,000 per kilogram.

- The average chocolate bar contains insect fragments due to the difficulty of keeping cocoa beans insect-free.

- Some people have a genetic mutation that prevents them from tasting bitter flavors like those in broccoli and Brussels sprouts.

- The practice of toasting with drinks originated from the ancient Romans, who put toast in wine to improve flavor.

- The Hass avocado, known for its creamy flesh, originated from a single tree planted by Rudolph Hass in California in the 1920s.

- Peanuts are not true nuts but legumes that grow underground and are related to beans.

- The Guinness World Record for the largest pizza was set with a pizza measuring over 13,500 square feet in Italy.

- Sushi does not traditionally include salmon; it became popular in Japan after Norwegian businessmen introduced it in the 1980s.

- Watermelons are more than 90% water, making them excellent for hydration.

- The world's hottest chili pepper, the Carolina Reaper, can reach over 2 million Scoville Heat Units.

- The ice cream cone was reportedly invented at the 1904 World's Fair by Ernest Hamwi when he rolled a waffle to hold ice cream.

- In Japan, square watermelons are grown for easier stacking and storage, but they are more expensive.

- The average American eats about 25 pounds of candy annually, with the majority consumed around Halloween.

- Ketchup was originally marketed as a medicine in the 1830s to treat indigestion and diarrhea.

- The artichoke we eat is the flower bud of a thistle plant, harvested before it blooms.

- The largest chocolate bar ever made weighed over 12,000 pounds and was created in the UK.

- Mangoes are considered the king of fruits in India and are the national fruit.

- Mayonnaise is a traditional ingredient in Japanese cuisine and is often used as a topping for pizza.

- Edible gold leaf, used to decorate desserts, is considered non-toxic and safe for consumption.

- The world's most expensive burger is made with wagyu beef, foie gras, and truffles, costing over $5,000.

- In Iceland, hákarl is a traditional dish made from fermented shark that has been buried and dried for months.

- The Caesar salad was not named after Julius Caesar but after its inventor, Caesar Cardini, a restaurateur.

- The fungus truffle is considered a delicacy due to its unique aroma and can cost thousands of dollars per pound.

- Lobsters were once considered peasant food and were so abundant that they were used as fertilizer.

- The capsaicin in chili peppers triggers endorphin release, creating a pleasurable sensation similar to a "runner's high."

- Chewing gum does not take seven years to digest but passes through the digestive system like any other food.

- The pistil of a flower eventually forms the fruit, and the ovules inside the pistil become seeds.

- The pretzel was supposedly created by monks in the Middle Ages to resemble arms crossed in prayer.

- Some cheeses, like Limburger, have bacteria similar to those found on human skin, which contribute to their distinct smell.

- Figs are technically inverted flowers, pollinated by tiny wasps that often become trapped inside the fruit.

- In Switzerland, fondue became a popular dish to promote the consumption of excess cheese during World War II.

- Wasabi is usually replaced by horseradish in sushi restaurants because real wasabi is expensive and difficult to grow.

- The most expensive coffee, Kopi Luwak, is made using beans digested and excreted by civet cats.

- Maple syrup is made from the sap of sugar maples and requires over 40 gallons of sap to produce one gallon of syrup.

- The world's largest omelet weighed over 14,000 pounds and was made in Portugal with 145,000 eggs.

- There are more than 7,500 varieties of apples grown worldwide, with thousands of flavors and colors.

- Worcestershire sauce was originally created as a recipe brought back from India, later adapted to British tastes.

- The banana is the most popular fruit in the world, with over 100 billion eaten annually.

- Popcorn kernels pop because of the water trapped inside, which turns to steam and explodes the outer shell.

- Some species of jellyfish are considered delicacies in Asia and are prepared as dried snacks or salads.

- Croissants are not originally French but were first made in Austria and brought to France by Marie Antoinette.

- Rice is a staple food for over half of the world's population, particularly in Asia and Africa.

- The world's largest lollipop weighed over 7,000 pounds and was made in California.

- White chocolate is not technically chocolate, as it lacks cocoa solids and is made from cocoa butter.

- Chia seeds were a staple in the diets of ancient Aztec and Mayan warriors for their energy-boosting properties.

- Apples contain a natural chemical called malic acid that helps remove stains from teeth.

- The world's most expensive ice cream sundae, costing over $1,000, is topped with edible gold and rare chocolate.

- Cucumbers contain more than 95% water, making them extremely hydrating and low-calorie snacks.

- The term "toast" originated in ancient Rome, where bread was dropped into wine to improve flavor.

- French fries were likely invented in Belgium, where villagers fried fish and potatoes in the 1600s.

- Oyster sauce was invented accidentally by Lee Kum Sheung when he overcooked oysters and turned them into a paste.

- The most expensive tea, Da Hong Pao, is grown in China and can cost up to $1,400 per gram.

- The word "whiskey" comes from the Gaelic term meaning "water of life."

- The world's largest fruit salad weighed over 22,000 pounds and contained more than 20 types of fruit.

- Root beer was originally made from sarsaparilla root and was used as a medicinal tonic.

- Caviar is considered a delicacy but was once served to fishermen and peasants as a cheap food source.

- Peanut butter was first introduced at the St. Louis World's Fair in 1904.

- Cheese is believed to have been discovered accidentally when milk stored in animal stomachs curdled into solid form.

- Macadamia nuts are the most expensive nuts due to their slow-growing trees and delicate harvesting process.

- Sushi chefs must undergo years of training before they can serve the poisonous pufferfish (fugu) safely.

- The world's largest sushi roll measured over 8,000 feet in length and was made in Japan.

- Cinnamon was once considered more valuable than gold and was traded extensively in ancient times.

- The first chocolate bar was created by combining cocoa powder, sugar, and cocoa butter in the 1800s.

- Tofu, made from coagulated soy milk, originated in China over 2,000 years ago.

- The world's longest hot dog was over 200 feet long and made in Paraguay.

- Pesto, a traditional Italian sauce, is made by grinding basil, garlic, pine nuts, and Parmesan cheese.

- Cheese fondue is believed to have originated in Switzerland as a way to use leftover cheese and bread.

- Soy sauce, a staple in Asian cuisine, is made from fermented soybeans, wheat, salt, and water.

- The carrot cake became popular in the U.S. during World War II due to the rationing of sugar.

- The durian fruit is considered the "king of fruits" in Southeast Asia but has a strong odor some people dislike.

- Fermented foods like kimchi and sauerkraut were initially made to preserve vegetables through winter.

- Couscous is a traditional North African dish made from steamed semolina wheat granules.

- Popcorn became popular during the Great Depression because it was an affordable snack.

- The world's largest gingerbread house measured over 39,000 cubic feet and was built in Texas.

- Most wasabi served outside of Japan is actually horseradish dyed green due to the high cost of real wasabi.

- Olive oil, a staple of Mediterranean cuisine, is often used to marinate vegetables and add flavor to dishes.

- The croissant's crescent shape was originally created to commemorate the victory over the Ottoman Empire.

- The fig has a symbiotic relationship with fig wasps, which pollinate its flowers while laying eggs inside.

- The world's largest chocolate sculpture weighed over 10,000 pounds and was created in Belgium.

- Pancakes are one of the oldest breakfast foods, dating back to prehistoric times.

- Pop-Tarts, a popular breakfast pastry, were originally designed to be an easy-to-make treat requiring no refrigeration.

- Seaweed is a staple in Japanese cuisine and is often used to wrap sushi and add flavor to soups.

- The French omelet is made by quickly cooking beaten eggs in butter until just set and then folded.

- The world's largest peanut butter and jelly sandwich weighed over 1,400 pounds.

- Indian curry is a blend of spices like turmeric, cumin, and coriander that dates back thousands of years.

- Bubble tea originated in Taiwan and is known for its chewy tapioca pearls and sweet tea base.

- The world's largest chocolate fountain is over 26 feet tall and was created in Las Vegas.

- Traditional Italian balsamic vinegar is aged in barrels for up to 25 years.

- Noodles are believed to have originated in China over 4,000 years ago, as evidenced by an archaeological find.

- Kiwifruit was originally known as Chinese gooseberry before being marketed as kiwi by New Zealand growers.

- The world's largest cheese platter weighed over 4,000 pounds and was created in France.

- Chiles en nogada is a Mexican dish traditionally made with poblano peppers, a walnut-based sauce, and pomegranate seeds.

- Vietnamese pho is a traditional noodle soup with herbs, meat, and spices, often served as breakfast.

- The world's largest pizza delivery was made from South Africa to Australia, covering over 6,500 miles.

- Greek yogurt is strained to remove excess whey, giving it a thicker consistency than regular yogurt.

- Pad Thai, a popular Thai noodle dish, often includes shrimp, peanuts, and bean sprouts.

- The most expensive tea cup, made from jadeite, was sold for over $30 million at an auction.

- In Malaysia, nasi lemak is a traditional dish of rice cooked in coconut milk, served with sambal and eggs.

- Sweetened condensed milk was created in the 19th century to preserve milk for long periods without refrigeration.

- Currywurst, a popular German fast food, consists of sliced sausage topped with curry ketchup.

- Pavlova, a meringue-based dessert named after a Russian ballerina, is claimed by both New Zealand and Australia.

- The world's largest sushi mosaic was made with over 20,000 pieces of sushi in Norway.

- German sauerkraut is made by fermenting cabbage with salt and is known for its tangy flavor.

- Italian risotto is made by slowly cooking rice in broth, creating a creamy and comforting dish.

- The world's longest candy necklace measured over 4,000 feet and was made in the UK.

- Haggis, a traditional Scottish dish, is made from sheep's organs mixed with oatmeal and spices.

- Swiss raclette is a cheese traditionally melted and served over potatoes and pickles.

- A full English breakfast often includes eggs, bacon, sausage, beans, and grilled tomatoes.

- French macarons are made with almond flour and meringue, creating a delicate and colorful sandwich cookie.

- Tiramisu, an Italian dessert, is made with layers of coffee-soaked ladyfingers and mascarpone cream.

- The world's largest jigsaw gingerbread house was built in New York and used over 5,000 gingerbread pieces.

- Soy sauce originated over 2,500 years ago in China, and its fermentation process can take up to six months.

- Black truffles are among the world's most expensive foods, fetching prices of over $1,000 per pound due to their scarcity and unique flavor.

- The world's hottest chili, the Carolina Reaper, was cultivated in South Carolina and can cause severe burning sensations.

- Maple syrup production requires warm days and freezing nights to get the sap flowing from sugar maples.

- Cheese consumption per capita is highest in Denmark, where the average person consumes over 60 pounds per year.

- The McDonald's McRib sandwich is only periodically available due to the fluctuating cost of pork.

- Cucumber slices are often placed over eyes in beauty treatments because they have cooling and anti-inflammatory properties.

Inventions and Inventors

- Thomas Edison, known for inventing the light bulb, held over 1,000 patents, including ones for the phonograph and motion picture camera.

- Nikola Tesla envisioned wireless power transmission, and his work laid the groundwork for modern wireless communication.

- The Wright brothers flew the first powered airplane in 1903 after testing numerous gliders and propellers.

- Johannes Gutenberg's invention of the printing press in the 15th century revolutionized the distribution of knowledge.

- Alexander Graham Bell's invention of the telephone was originally intended as a device to assist the deaf.

- George Washington Carver developed over 300 uses for peanuts, including dyes, plastics, and gasoline.

- The invention of paper is credited to the ancient Chinese, who used plant fibers around 105 CE.

- Tim Berners-Lee created the World Wide Web in 1989 while working at CERN, transforming global communication.

- The concept of the assembly line, introduced by Henry Ford, revolutionized mass production and made cars more affordable.

- Eli Whitney's cotton gin greatly increased cotton production but also inadvertently expanded slavery in the U.S.

- Stephanie Kwolek invented Kevlar, a strong synthetic fiber used in bulletproof vests and protective gear.

- Alexander Fleming discovered penicillin in 1928, which became the world's first antibiotic and changed medicine.

- Louis Pasteur developed pasteurization, a process that kills bacteria in milk and wine to make them safe to consume.

- The transistor, invented by John Bardeen, Walter Brattain, and William Shockley, is the basis of modern electronic devices.

- Charles Goodyear's vulcanization process made rubber more durable and useful for tires and various products.

- Garrett Morgan, an African-American inventor, created a traffic signal with a third position for caution, leading to modern traffic lights.

- Percy Spencer invented the microwave oven after discovering that microwaves could melt chocolate in his pocket.

- Leonardo da Vinci conceptualized the helicopter, parachute, and other inventions, centuries before they were built.

- The first vaccine, created by Edward Jenner, was made for smallpox after observing that milkmaids exposed to cowpox were immune.

- Rudolf Diesel invented the diesel engine, which runs on a more efficient fuel than gasoline.

- Josephine Cochrane invented the first automatic dishwasher in the 1880s to wash fine china faster.

- James Naismith invented basketball in 1891 to keep his students active during the winter months.

- The zipper was invented by Whitcomb L. Judson, but Gideon Sundback improved it into the design we use today.

- Mary Anderson invented the windshield wiper after noticing streetcar drivers struggling to see in the rain.

- Grace Hopper developed the first computer compiler, which made it easier to program computers using English-like commands.

- Samuel Morse developed Morse code and invented the telegraph, revolutionizing long-distance communication.

- The light-emitting diode (LED) was invented by Nick Holonyak Jr. in 1962 and is now used in many electronic devices.

- The ballpoint pen was invented by László Bíró to improve ink flow and avoid smudging.

- Bette Nesmith Graham invented liquid paper, the first correction fluid, to fix typing errors quickly.

- The computer mouse was invented by Douglas Engelbart, who also pioneered early internet concepts.

- John Harrison created marine chronometers that solved the problem of calculating longitude at sea.

- The flushing toilet was improved upon by Thomas Crapper, who popularized it and patented related plumbing fixtures.

- Fritz Haber and Carl Bosch developed the process for synthesizing ammonia, essential for fertilizers and explosives.

- Edwin Land invented the Polaroid instant camera, which revolutionized photography.

- Karl Benz is credited with inventing the modern automobile with an internal combustion engine in the 1880s.

- Hedy Lamarr, a Hollywood actress, co-invented frequency-hopping technology, leading to modern wireless communication.

- Elisha Otis invented the safety elevator, allowing for safer and taller skyscrapers.

- The photocopier was invented by Chester Carlson, making duplication of documents easier for businesses.

- The World Wide Web Consortium (W3C), led by Tim Berners-Lee, sets the standards for web development.

- John Logie Baird invented the first working television, capable of broadcasting moving images over the air.

- The hypodermic syringe was invented by Charles Pravaz and Alexander Wood, making injections more precise.

- Wilson Greatbatch invented the implantable pacemaker, which helps regulate abnormal heart rhythms.

- Nils Bohlin invented the three-point seat belt, now standard in vehicles and responsible for saving millions of lives.

- The Richter scale, used to measure earthquake magnitude, was developed by Charles Richter in 1935.

- Thomas C. Richards invented the first metal detector, used to find unexploded ordnance after World War II.

- The anemometer, a device used to measure wind speed, was invented by Leon Battista Alberti in the 15th century.

- The invention of the can opener came nearly 50 years after the invention of canned food.

- The phonograph, invented by Edison, was the first device to record and play back sound.

- Marie Curie, known for her pioneering research on radioactivity, was the first woman to win a Nobel Prize.

- The Braille system, used by the visually impaired to read and write, was invented by Louis Braille at age 15.

- Gutenberg's printing press used movable type, allowing for mass production of books and reducing their cost.

- The first commercially available electric vacuum cleaner was invented by Hubert Cecil Booth.

- Philo Farnsworth developed the first fully functional all-electronic television system in the 1920s.

- The integrated circuit, crucial for modern electronics, was developed independently by Jack Kilby and Robert Noyce.

- George Eastman made photography more accessible by developing roll film and the Kodak camera.

- The safety razor with replaceable blades was patented by King Camp Gillette, leading to a global brand.

- Thomas Savery and Thomas Newcomen developed the first practical steam engines for pumping water from mines.

- The concept of synthetic dyes began with William Henry Perkin's accidental discovery of mauveine in 1856.

- Richard Drew invented masking tape and Scotch tape while working at 3M in the 1920s.

- The polygraph, or lie detector, was invented by John A. Larson to detect physiological changes when lying.

- The tuning fork, used in musical instruments and medical testing, was invented by John Shore in 1711.

- Guglielmo Marconi is credited with developing radio telegraphy, leading to the first transatlantic radio transmission.

- Blaise Pascal invented the first mechanical calculator in the 17th century to assist with arithmetic calculations.

- The vacuum flask, commonly known as a Thermos, was invented by Sir James Dewar for scientific experiments.

- Joseph Priestley is credited with discovering oxygen and developing carbonated water, the precursor to soda.

- The artificial heart was first implanted in a human by Robert Jarvik in the 1980s.

- Clarence Birdseye revolutionized frozen food with his quick-freezing process, preserving taste and nutrients.

- Wilhelm Röntgen discovered X-rays, which led to their widespread use in medical imaging.

- The modern computer operating system was pioneered by Dennis Ritchie and Ken Thompson in the 1970s.

- The phonetic alphabet, as we know it today, was developed by the International Civil Aviation Organization.

Planets and Space

- The sun is composed of over 99.8% of the total mass in our solar system and is primarily made of hydrogen and helium.

- A day on Venus is longer than a Venusian year due to its slow rotation, taking 243 Earth days to complete one rotation.

- The moon is slowly drifting away from Earth at about 1.5 inches per year, affecting the tides and Earth's rotation over millions of years.

- Mars has the largest volcano in the solar system, Olympus Mons, which is nearly 13.6 miles high and about the size of Arizona.

- Jupiter's Great Red Spot is a storm larger than Earth that has been raging for over 300 years.

- Neptune's winds are the fastest in the solar system, reaching speeds of over 1,200 mph.

- Mercury experiences extreme temperature fluctuations due to its thin atmosphere, with daytime temperatures reaching 800°F and nighttime dropping to -290°F.

- Saturn's moon Titan has lakes and rivers of liquid methane, as its surface temperature is too cold for liquid water.

- The sun's core reaches temperatures of up to 27 million °F, where nuclear fusion converts hydrogen into helium.

- Pluto, reclassified as a dwarf planet, has five known moons, with Charon being the largest, almost half Pluto's size.

- Space officially begins at the Kármán line, 62 miles above Earth's surface.

- The Milky Way galaxy contains an estimated 100 billion stars and is part of a group called the Local Group.

- The Andromeda galaxy, the nearest spiral galaxy to us, will collide with the Milky Way in about 4.5 billion years.

- Uranus rotates on its side, with its poles facing the sun rather than its equator, possibly due to a collision with another object.

- Comets have two tails: one made of dust and the other of ionized gases, both pointing away from the sun due to solar wind.

- Black holes form when massive stars collapse under their own gravity, creating regions where gravity is so strong that not even light can escape.

- Space is not completely empty but filled with trace particles, cosmic rays, and cosmic microwave background radiation.

- The largest moon in our solar system, Ganymede, is bigger than Mercury and has its own magnetic field.

- The International Space Station orbits Earth at a speed of 17,500 mph, circling the planet about 16 times a day.

- Venus is the hottest planet in the solar system, with surface temperatures exceeding 860°F due to a runaway greenhouse effect.

- Earth's atmosphere protects us from harmful solar and cosmic radiation while also burning up most meteoroids.

- The James Webb Space Telescope, designed to replace Hubble, will provide unprecedented views of the early universe.

- Saturn's rings are composed of billions of ice particles and are thought to be remnants of a shattered moon.

- The surface of Mars contains iron oxide, giving it the characteristic red color known as "The Red Planet."

- Voyager 1, launched in 1977, is now the farthest human-made object from Earth, exploring interstellar space.

- The sun's activity, known as the solar cycle, peaks every 11 years, resulting in increased sunspots and solar flares.

- The surface gravity on Mars is only about 38% that of Earth, meaning you would weigh much less on Mars.

- Jupiter has 92 known moons, the most of any planet, including the four largest, known as the Galilean moons.

- Water has been detected on the moon and Mars, which could be used by future space missions.

- The sun's magnetic field is responsible for the solar wind, which creates the beautiful auroras on Earth's poles.

- Astronauts in space grow up to 2 inches taller due to the lack of gravity compressing their spines.

- One day on Jupiter takes just under 10 hours, making it the fastest-spinning planet in the solar system.

- The Kuiper Belt, a region beyond Neptune, contains thousands of small icy bodies, including Pluto.

- The asteroid belt between Mars and Jupiter is believed to contain remnants of a failed planet.

- Saturn is the least dense planet, with a density low enough that it could theoretically float in water.

- Cosmic rays are high-energy particles originating outside the solar system and can be harmful to astronauts.

- The Hubble Space Telescope has captured images from more than 13 billion light-years away, revealing early galaxies.

- The lunar regolith (moon dust) is highly abrasive and can damage equipment, presenting a challenge for future lunar missions.

- Neutron stars are incredibly dense objects formed from collapsed supernovae, with a sugar-cube-sized portion weighing billions of tons.

- The Oort Cloud is a hypothesized shell of icy objects surrounding our solar system, thought to be the source of long-period comets.

- The hottest star types, known as O-type stars, can reach temperatures above 70,000°F and have relatively short lifespans.

- The first exoplanet discovered was 51 Pegasi b in 1995, orbiting a star similar to the sun.

- The Valles Marineris canyon system on Mars is over 2,500 miles long, dwarfing the Grand Canyon.

- Lunar eclipses occur when Earth passes between the sun and moon, casting a reddish shadow on the moon.

- The term "supermoon" describes a full moon that appears larger because it is closer to Earth in its orbit.

- Quasars are extremely luminous objects fueled by supermassive black holes, emitting more energy than entire galaxies.

- The term "gravity assist" refers to spacecraft using a planet's gravity to change speed or trajectory.

- Europa, one of Jupiter's moons, is thought to have a subsurface ocean beneath its icy crust, raising the possibility of life.

- The sun is classified as a G-type main-sequence star and will eventually expand into a red giant in about 5 billion years.

- Triton, Neptune's largest moon, has geysers that erupt nitrogen gas, suggesting possible subsurface heating.

- Meteor showers occur when Earth passes through the debris left behind by comets, creating brilliant light displays.

- Proxima Centauri is the closest known star to Earth besides the sun, at about 4.24 light-years away.

- Saturn's moon Enceladus has geysers that spew water vapor and ice particles, hinting at an ocean beneath the ice.

- Mercury has almost no atmosphere, leading to extreme temperature differences between its day and night sides.

- The "Pale Blue Dot" photo, taken by Voyager 1, shows Earth as a tiny speck in the vastness of space.

- The Kuiper Belt is home to dwarf planets like Pluto, Haumea, Makemake, and Eris.

- The Great Attractor is a gravitational anomaly influencing the motion of thousands of galaxies, including the Milky Way.

- Spacecraft electronics must be specially shielded to protect against cosmic rays and the vacuum of space.

- The Large Magellanic Cloud is a satellite galaxy of the Milky Way and is visible from the Southern Hemisphere.

- The Horsehead Nebula, named for its distinctive shape, is a region of gas and dust in the Orion constellation.

- Methane lakes and rivers on Titan are replenished by rain from the moon's nitrogen-methane atmosphere.

- Space probes like New Horizons, sent to explore the outer solar system, rely on radioisotope thermoelectric generators for power.

- Black holes can grow in size by accreting matter from nearby stars or merging with other black holes.

- Solar sails are a theoretical propulsion system that uses sunlight to push spacecraft, similar to how wind pushes sailboats.

- Uranus was the first planet discovered using a telescope and was originally mistaken for a star.

- SpaceX and Blue Origin have developed reusable rockets that have significantly reduced the cost of space travel.

- Voyager 2 is the only spacecraft to have flown by all four outer planets (Jupiter, Saturn, Uranus, and Neptune).

- The Gemini and Apollo programs demonstrated spacewalking, docking, and other techniques necessary for moon missions.

- Saturn's hexagon-shaped storm at its north pole is an unexplained phenomenon first observed by Voyager.

- The "dark side of the moon" is a misnomer, as all sides receive sunlight; it's simply the side that faces away from Earth.

- Solar flares and coronal mass ejections can disrupt satellite communications and power grids on Earth.

- Liquid water cannot exist on Mars' surface due to its thin atmosphere and low pressure, but briny liquid might persist underground.

- The Parker Solar Probe, launched in 2018, will come closer to the sun than any previous spacecraft to study the corona.

- Mars rovers like Curiosity and Perseverance have provided detailed information on the planet's surface and geology.

- The sun's light takes approximately 8 minutes and 20 seconds to reach Earth, traveling 93 million miles.

- Dark matter and dark energy, which we cannot directly observe, are believed to make up most of the universe.

- Triton orbits Neptune in the opposite direction of the planet's rotation, suggesting it was captured by Neptune's gravity.

- An astronaut's body undergoes significant changes in microgravity, including muscle atrophy and loss of bone density.

- The Event Horizon Telescope collaboration captured the first-ever image of a black hole in the M87 galaxy.

- Mars experiences dust storms that can engulf the entire planet and last for weeks, reducing solar power generation.

- Most meteors burn up in Earth's atmosphere, with only a small fraction reaching the ground as meteorites.

Famous People of the Past

- Cleopatra was reputedly the first known victim of an asp bite, traditionally believed to have been delivered by a poisonous Egyptian cobra.

- Albert Einstein developed the theory of relativity, which fundamentally changed our understanding of physics and introduced the iconic equation, $E=mc^2$, describing the relationship between mass and energy. Although most famous for his theoretical work, Einstein was offered the presidency of Israel in 1952 but declined the honor, saying he was not suited for politics.

- Napoleon Bonaparte was once attacked by a horde of rabbits during a hunting trip organized in 1807 by his chief of staff.

- Julius Caesar was kidnapped by pirates when he was around 25 years old and later raised a fleet to capture them.

- Mozart composed a piece titled "Leck mich im Arsch," which translates to "Lick me in the ass," as a humorous canon.

- Genghis Khan rarely bathed because he believed it was harmful to one's health, but he was very concerned about personal hygiene.

- Queen Elizabeth The First had a lifelong fear of marriage, possibly influenced by her father's tumultuous love life and her mother's fate.

- Vincent van Gogh only sold one painting during his lifetime.

- Christopher Columbus never set foot on the land that is now the United States during his explorations.

- Albert Einstein never wore socks, considering them unnecessary and unpleasant.

- Leonardo da Vinci was left-handed and wrote his notes from right to left in mirror writing.

- Alexander the Great was fascinated by medicine and often diagnosed his soldiers' ailments.

- Sir Isaac Newton had a dog named Diamond, who once knocked over a candle and caused a fire that destroyed many of Newton's papers.

- Marie Antoinette never said, "Let them eat cake." The phrase was falsely attributed to her during the French Revolution.

- Henry VIII of England had a collection of over 2,000 tapestries.

- Socrates claimed to have a personal Deamon who would warn him against mistakes but never tell him what to do.

- Joan of Arc began hearing voices at the age of 13, which she believed to be messages from God.

- Michelangelo was known to be temperamental and had a habit of destroying his own work out of frustration.

- Queen Victoria was a carrier of hemophilia, a genetic disorder that affected several royal families in Europe. Hemophilia is an inherited bleeding disorder in which the blood does not clot properly.

- Leonardo da Vinci dissected over 30 human corpses to study anatomy and physiology.

- Charles Darwin suffered from a fear of enclosed spaces, known as claustrophobia.

- Joan of Arc was captured by the Burgundians, sold to the English, and later burned at the stake for heresy.

- Edgar Allan Poe married his 13-year-old cousin, Virginia Clemm, when he was 27 years old.

- Galileo Galilei was placed under house arrest by the Catholic Church for promoting the heliocentric model of the universe.

- Thomas Edison was afraid of the dark and always slept with a light on.

- Cleopatra spoke several languages fluently, including Egyptian, Greek, and Latin.

- Napoleon Bonaparte was once saved from an assassination attempt by his mistress, Josephine.

- Despite his immense scientific contributions, Albert Einstein initially struggled in his early academic career and couldn't find a teaching job after graduating due to his unconventional methods.

- Queen Elizabeth The First was known for her love of sugar, which caused her teeth to blacken over time.

- Benjamin Franklin practiced vegetarianism for most of his life and believed it contributed to his health and longevity.

- Isaac Newton invented the cat flap, a small opening in a door for cats to pass through.

- Marie Curie's notebooks from her research on radioactivity are still radioactive and are stored in lead-lined boxes.

- Leonardo da Vinci designed plans for a flying machine, a tank, and a diving suit, among other inventions.

- Genghis Khan was rumored to have had green eyes and red hair, unusual traits for someone of Mongolian descent.

- Queen Elizabeth I survived several assassination attempts, including one involving poisoned gloves.

- Vincent van Gogh cut off his own ear during a fit of madness and later presented it to a prostitute.

- Charles Darwin was terrified of thunderstorms and would hide under his bed during storms.

- Joan of Arc dressed in men's clothing and claimed to have received visions from saints instructing her to lead the French army.

- Socrates was sentenced to death by drinking poison hemlock after being found guilty of corrupting the youth of Athens and impiety.

- Henry VIII of England had six wives, two of whom he had executed.

- Galileo Galilei was the first to observe the moons of Jupiter through a telescope.

- Cleopatra was the last active ruler of the Ptolemaic Kingdom of Egypt before it became a province of the Roman Empire.

- Genghis Khan's descendants are estimated to number in the millions today due to his extensive progeny, with genetic studies suggesting that about 16 million men worldwide can trace their Y-chromosome lineage back to him.

- Queen Elizabeth The First never married and was known as the "Virgin Queen" or "Good Queen Bess."

- Thomas Edison was partially deaf and attributed his hearing loss to a childhood bout of scarlet fever.

- Leonardo da Vinci was known for his vegetarianism and love of animals, often buying caged birds at the market just to set them free.

- Napoleon Bonaparte was known for his short stature, standing at around 5 feet 3 inches tall.

- Michelangelo was ambidextrous and could draw with both hands simultaneously.

- Socrates never wrote down any of his teachings, so much of what is known about him comes from the writings of his students, particularly Plato.

- Marie Curie was the first woman to win a Nobel Prize and remains the only person to win Nobel Prizes in two different scientific fields.

- Cleopatra was romantically involved with Julius Caesar and later Mark Antony, both of whom were powerful Roman leaders.

- Wolfgang Amadeus Mozart composed over 600 works in his lifetime, including symphonies, operas, and chamber music.

- Genghis Khan was responsible for the deaths of an estimated 40 million people during his military campaigns.

- Vincent van Gogh only began painting in his late 20s and produced over 2,000 artworks in less than a decade.

- Alexander the Great died at the age of 32 under mysterious circumstances, possibly from malaria or poisoning.

- Albert Einstein had a habit of forgetting appointments and would often rely on his wife, Mileva, to keep track of his schedule.

- Marie Antoinette was known for her extravagant spending and lavish lifestyle, which contributed to her unpopularity among the French people.

Famous People Today

- Oprah Winfrey's birth name is actually Orpah, but it was misspelled on her birth certificate. She once gave away 276 cars to her audience members during an episode of "The Oprah Winfrey Show." Oprah has a fear of chewing gum and won't allow it in her presence.

- Bill Gates scored 1590 out of 1600 on his SATs. Gates once released a jar full of mosquitoes during a TED Talk to draw attention to malaria prevention.

- Barack Obama collects Spider-Man and Conan the Barbarian comics. He was the first sitting president to visit a federal prison.

- Ellen DeGeneres once worked as a house painter and a vacuum cleaner salesperson. She is also extremely afraid of clowns.

- Jeff Bezos chose the name "Amazon" for his company because he wanted a name that started with the letter "A" to appear at the top of alphabetical lists. He briefly worked at McDonald's in high school.

- Warren Buffett, one of the richest people alive, still lives in the same house he bought in Omaha, Nebraska, in 1958 for $31,500.

- LeBron James spends over $1.5 million a year on his body, including cryotherapy and hyperbaric chambers. LeBron is part owner of Liverpool Football Club. James eats the same meal before every game: chicken, pasta with tomato sauce, and a salad with balsamic vinaigrette dressing.

- Michael Jordan has a fear of water and is not a good swimmer. He is the only player in NBA history to score 40 or more points at age 40 or older.

- Elon Musk taught himself computer programming at the age of 12 and sold a video game called "Blastar" for $500. He once planned to send a greenhouse to Mars with a miniature olive tree as the first life on the planet. Elon Musk does not only own the electric car company Tesla but he also owns a company called The Boring Company, which aims to dig tunnels for transportation systems.

- Mark Zuckerberg is red-green colorblind, which is why Facebook's primary color is blue. He built a "sleep box" for his wife to help with her sleep schedule as a new parent. Mark Zuckerberg's dog, Beast, has over 2.6 million followers on Facebook.

- Tom Hanks has an asteroid named after him: 12818 Tomhanks. Tom Hanks is also related to former President Abraham Lincoln through Lincoln's mother, Nancy Hanks.

- Serena Williams has a habit of bouncing her tennis ball five times before her first serve and twice before her second.

- Michael Phelps, the Olympic swimmer, eats 12,000 calories a day during training, including pizza and pasta.

- Cristiano Ronaldo sleeps in an oxygen chamber to aid muscle recovery.

- Taylor Swift's lucky number is 13. She was born on the 13th, turned 13 on a Friday the 13th, and her first album went gold in 13 weeks.

- Usain Bolt ate 1,000 chicken McNuggets during the 2008 Beijing Olympics.

- Adele graduated from the BRIT School for Performing Arts & Technology, along with classmates Jessie J and Leona Lewis.

- LeBron James spends over $1 million a year on maintaining his body, including cryotherapy and hyperbaric chambers.

- Katy Perry's real name is Katheryn Elizabeth Hudson. She changed it to avoid confusion with actress Kate Hudson.

- Justin Bieber can solve a Rubik's Cube in less than two minutes.

- Rihanna's hit song "Umbrella" was originally written for Britney Spears.

- Tiger Woods is a certified scuba diver and has gone diving in the Great Barrier Reef.

- Ariana Grande has a five-octave vocal range, spanning from a low B2 to a high Eb7.

- Novak Djokovic is known for his gluten-free diet, which he credits with improving his health and performance.

- Simone Biles has a condition called Attention Deficit Hyperactivity Disorder (ADHD), but it hasn't stopped her from becoming one of the greatest gymnasts of all time.

- Shakira speaks five languages: Spanish, English, Portuguese, Italian, and Arabic.

- Kobe Bryant won an Academy Award for Best Animated Short Film in 2018 for "Dear Basketball," based on a letter he wrote announcing his retirement from basketball.

- Kanye West worked as a telemarketer selling insurance before becoming a rapper.

- Usain Bolt's father named him after the famous 1970s Jamaican reggae musician, Lightning Bolt.

- Taylor Swift once won a national poetry contest with her poem "Monster in My Closet" when she was in the fourth grade.

- Kim Kardashian's first job was as a stylist for Paris Hilton.

- LeBron James eats the same meal before every game: chicken, pasta with tomato sauce, and a salad with balsamic vinaigrette dressing.

- Adele has a fear of stage fright and has vomited before many of her performances.

- Lady Gaga is the first artist to win a Golden Globe, Grammy, BAFTA, and Academy Award in the same year.

- Justin Bieber can play the drums, guitar, piano, and trumpet.

- Serena Williams has won more prize money than any other female athlete in history.

- Katy Perry once worked for the company Clueless, where she designed and sold clothes.

- Rihanna's song "S&M" was banned in 11 countries due to its suggestive lyrics.

- Tiger Woods has a black belt in Taekwondo.

- Ariana Grande is vegan and has been since 2013.

- Ed Sheeran is a big fan of ketchup and even has a bottle tattooed on his arm.

- Simone Biles has a condition called Ailurophobia, which is a fear of cats.

- Drake is a huge fan of Harry Potter and has a tattoo of the series' character, Hermione Granger.

- Cristiano Ronaldo has a museum dedicated to his life and career in his hometown of Funchal, Madeira.

- Beyoncé has a church named after her in San Francisco, called the "Beyoncé Mass."

- Lionel Messi has a rare disorder called growth hormone deficiency, which stunted his growth as a child.

- Shakira's hips don't lie; she has been trained in belly dancing since she was four years old.

- Kobe Bryant was fluent in Italian and Spanish.

- Nicki Minaj's alter ego, Roman Zolanski, is a British homosexual male.

- Roger Federer is a polyglot and can speak Swiss German, Standard German, French, and English fluently.

- Kanye West collects art and has a vast collection of contemporary and modern pieces.

- Usain Bolt's favorite food is yams, a popular dish in his native Jamaica.

- Taylor Swift's cat, Olivia Benson, is named after the character Mariska Hargitay plays on "Law & Order: SVU."

- Kim Kardashian once had a cameo in the film "Disaster Movie."

- LeBron James was once a contestant on the game show "The Price Is Right" but lost.

- Adele's favorite TV show is "The Walking Dead."

- Cristiano Ronaldo's favorite actor is Al Pacino.

- Lady Gaga is a big fan of horror movies and has said that they inspire her music.

- Justin Bieber has a fear of sharks.

- Serena Williams has a habit of bouncing her tennis ball five times before her first serve and twice before her second.

- Katy Perry collects antique baby carriages.

- Rihanna's first job was selling clothes in a street stall in Barbados.

- Tiger Woods is a skilled scuba diver and has explored coral reefs all over the world.

- Ariana Grande is a huge fan of the Harry Potter series and even owns a wand.

- Beyoncé has a fear of heights.

- Shakira's hips are insured for $1 billion.

- Kobe Bryant was a big fan of the movie "The Godfather" and even named his production company "Granity Studios" after it.

- Nicki Minaj is a huge fan of the cartoon character SpongeBob SquarePants.

- Roger Federer once served as a ball boy at the Swiss Indoors tennis tournament as a child.

- Kanye West owns a pair of slippers made from fox fur.

- Usain Bolt has scoliosis, a condition that causes the spine to curve sideways.

- Taylor Swift once accidentally released her own personal phone number to her fans in a music video.

- Kim Kardashian's favorite TV show is "The Golden Girls."

- LeBron James sleeps an average of 12 hours a day during the NBA season to help with recovery.

- Adele has a fear of seagulls.

- Cristiano Ronaldo is a practicing Catholic and has several tattoos related to his faith.

- Lady Gaga once appeared on "The Sopranos" as a member of the Soprano family.

- Justin Bieber once vomited onstage during a concert in Arizona.

- Serena Williams has a habit of packing her own food when she travels to tournaments.

- Katy Perry has a cat named Kitty Purry..

- Tiger Woods's favorite food is cheeseburgers.

- Ariana Grande's favorite animal is the sea otter.

- Ed Sheeran once accidentally hit Justin Bieber in the face with a golf club while intoxicated.

- Simone Biles can do a triple-twisting double backflip, a skill no other female gymnast has ever performed.

- Drake is a huge fan of the British television series "Top Boy" and helped revive it by becoming an executive producer.

- Beyoncé once accidentally set her hair on fire during a performance but continued singing without missing a beat.

- Lionel Messi has a condition called growth hormone deficiency, which required him to take growth hormone injections when he was younger.

- Shakira's song "Waka Waka (This Time for Africa)" is the best-selling World Cup song of all time.

- Kobe Bryant once scored 81 points in a single NBA game, the second-highest total in history.

- Nicki Minaj once tried to be a waitress but was fired on her first day for being rude to customers.

Psychology and Behavior

- People tend to walk in circles when lost, a behavior thought to be due to natural asymmetries in leg strength or stride.

- People tend to yawn more frequently when others around them yawn, a phenomenon known as contagious yawning.

- Humans are more likely to remember unfinished tasks than completed ones, a phenomenon called the Zeigarnik effect.

- "The IKEA effect" makes people value things they assemble themselves more highly than ready-made items.

- People are more likely to overestimate their abilities when they have little knowledge of a topic, known as the Dunning-Kruger effect.

- We often pick the middle option when presented with three choices due to a psychological phenomenon called the compromise effect.

- When people laugh in groups, they tend to look at the person they feel closest to.

- We are more likely to say yes to a favor if someone has already done us a favor, known as the reciprocity principle.

- Individuals are more prone to buying something if they touch it, especially with high-texture or luxury items.

- "The spotlight effect" makes people believe they're being noticed more than they actually are.

- People unconsciously mimic the gestures and expressions of others to build rapport, known as the chameleon effect.

- Humans are more likely to repeat behaviors that are rewarded and avoid those that lead to punishment, known as operant conditioning.

- People tend to think more creatively when they are tired or during non-peak hours because of reduced self-censorship.

- When given limited options, people often experience choice overload and avoid making a decision altogether.

- People are more likely to buy items if the price is just below a round number, such as $19.99 instead of $20.

- In stressful situations, people often seek comfort food or nostalgic activities from their childhood.

- We tend to believe others are more influenced by media or persuasion than we are, known as the third-person effect.

- People often underestimate the impact of subtle environmental factors on their behavior, a phenomenon called priming.

- Humans are more likely to conform to group opinions even if they initially disagree, a tendency known as groupthink.

- We often overestimate how much others share our beliefs and preferences, known as the false consensus effect.

- People generally underestimate the time it will take to complete a task, known as the planning fallacy.

- Humans are more likely to feel satisfied with a decision if it is difficult or irreversible due to post-decision dissonance.

- "The mere exposure effect" makes people like something simply because they see it frequently.

- When someone tells a joke in a group, others tend to laugh more loudly and longer if they are fond of that person.

- Humans tend to assume that people who are attractive also possess other positive traits, called the halo effect.

- People often believe their memories are more accurate than they are, due to the reconstructive nature of memory.

- We tend to feel more confident about our own choices when others make similar ones, known as social proof.

- People are more likely to avoid losses than pursue gains, a concept known as loss aversion.

- "The foot-in-the-door technique" increases compliance by asking for a small favor first before a larger one.

- People are more likely to change their behavior when they receive positive reinforcement rather than punishment.

- We often attribute others' behavior to their personality while attributing our own to situational factors, known as fundamental attribution error.

- Humans tend to overvalue possessions simply because they own them, known as the endowment effect.

- People are more likely to agree with a message if it aligns with their existing beliefs due to confirmation bias.

- When people are part of a group, they are less likely to help someone in distress because of the diffusion of responsibility.

- Humans are generally bad at predicting their own future emotions, known as affective forecasting errors.

- People are more likely to follow through with goals if they make them specific and write them down.

- We tend to overestimate how much people notice our mistakes or flaws, a phenomenon known as the spotlight effect.

- Humans often prefer to continue with familiar routines and activities even if better alternatives are available due to the status quo bias.

- People tend to interpret ambiguous information in ways that support their existing beliefs, known as motivated reasoning.

- Humans are more prone to help others when they are in a positive mood because of a phenomenon called the feel-good, do-good effect.

- "The framing effect" means people will react differently to the same information depending on how it's presented.

- People tend to perceive neutral expressions as negative when they're in a bad mood, a phenomenon called emotional congruence.

- Humans are more likely to accept a delayed reward if it is framed as a bonus rather than a loss.

- When presented with limited information, people often make quick judgments based on stereotypes or past experiences.

- People are more likely to be dishonest when they're in dimly lit environments, as it provides a sense of anonymity.

- Individuals tend to follow group norms even when they're counter to their own beliefs due to a need for social approval.

- People are more likely to misremember events if they're presented with misleading information afterward, known as the misinformation effect.

- "The cheerleader effect" is the tendency to perceive people as more attractive when they are in groups rather than alone.

- People are more likely to trust those who display warmth and friendliness, even if they lack competence.

- Humans have an innate desire to resolve uncertainty, often leading to curiosity and risk-taking behavior.

- People often find it easier to recall information that matches their current mood due to mood-congruent memory.

Geography and Continents

- Africa is the only continent that is crossed by the equator, the Prime Meridian, and the Tropics of Cancer and Capricorn.

- Asia is home to the world's two most populous countries, China and India, together accounting for over a third of the global population.

- The Dead Sea, situated between Jordan and Israel, is the lowest point on land, lying 1,410 feet below sea level.

- Mount Everest, the world's tallest peak, sits on the border of Nepal and China and continues to grow each year due to shifting tectonic plates.

- Antarctica is the coldest, driest, and windiest continent and has no permanent human inhabitants.

- South America's Amazon River discharges more water than any other river, contributing about 20% of the world's freshwater runoff.

- Europe is the second smallest continent, but it has the most developed rail network, connecting almost every city by train.

- The Sahara Desert in Africa is the largest hot desert, roughly the size of the U.S., but it was once a lush, green area.

- The Great Barrier Reef off Australia's coast is the largest coral reef system and can be seen from space.

- North America is home to the world's largest freshwater lake, Lake Superior, by surface area.

- Australia is the only continent that is also a country, containing unique wildlife like kangaroos and koalas.

- The Mariana Trench in the Pacific Ocean is the world's deepest point, plunging nearly 36,000 feet.

- Europe's longest river, the Volga, flows entirely through Russia and is vital for transportation and irrigation.

- Greenland is the largest island on Earth, not considered a continent, and is mostly covered by an ice sheet.

- Africa is believed to be the birthplace of humanity, with fossil evidence of early hominids dating back millions of years.

- South America's Andes Mountains are the longest continental mountain range, extending over 4,300 miles.

- The Arctic Circle contains parts of eight countries, but no country fully owns the North Pole.

- Australia's Uluru (Ayers Rock) is one of the world's largest monoliths and a sacred site for Indigenous Australians.

- Asia is the largest continent by land area and accounts for about 60% of the world's population.

- North America's longest river, the Mississippi, has a watershed covering over 40% of the contiguous U.S.

- South America's Angel Falls is the world's tallest uninterrupted waterfall, plunging over 3,200 feet.

- Europe's Vatican City is the smallest independent state, both in population and size, with just about 800 residents.

- The highest point in Africa is Mount Kilimanjaro, a dormant volcano standing at 19,341 feet.

- Antarctica contains roughly 70% of the world's freshwater as ice, although none of its glaciers are named.

- The Ural Mountains in Russia are considered the natural boundary between Europe and Asia.

- Asia's Gobi Desert is one of the world's largest deserts, stretching across northern China and Mongolia.

- The Great Rift Valley in Africa is a geologic formation caused by tectonic forces, extending from Lebanon to Mozambique.

- Europe's Alps are home to many ski resorts and include Mont Blanc, the tallest peak in Western Europe.

- The Amazon Rainforest is the largest tropical rainforest, covering over 2.1 million square miles in nine South American countries.

- Africa has the most countries of any continent, with 54 recognized nations.

- New Zealand's Fiordland National Park is one of the world's largest fiords, formed by ancient glaciers.

- The Danube River flows through ten European countries, making it the most international river in the world.

- South Africa has three capital cities: Pretoria (administrative), Cape Town (legislative), and Bloemfontein (judicial).

- The Australian Outback is a sparsely populated region known for its rugged beauty and unique wildlife.

- Asia's Caspian Sea is the world's largest enclosed inland body of water, often considered both a lake and a sea.

- Europe's Eiffel Tower in Paris was initially criticized but is now one of the most visited monuments in the world.

- The Atacama Desert in Chile is one of the driest places on Earth, receiving less than 0.6 inches of rainfall annually.

- North America's Grand Canyon, carved by the Colorado River, is over a mile deep in some places.

- Antarctica has an active volcano, Mount Erebus, which is one of the few volcanoes with a permanent lava lake.

- Asia's Lake Baikal is the world's deepest freshwater lake, reaching depths of over 5,300 feet.

- Mount Fuji is Japan's highest peak and a national symbol, often depicted in art and literature.

- Europe's Black Forest in Germany is known for its dense trees and was the inspiration for many Brothers Grimm fairy tales.

- South America's Pantanal is the world's largest tropical wetland, supporting diverse wildlife like jaguars and caimans.

- The Himalayas, which span five countries in Asia, contain ten of the world's fourteen highest peaks.

- Greenland's ice sheet is melting rapidly, contributing significantly to rising global sea levels.

- The Galapagos Islands, located in the Pacific Ocean, are home to many unique species that helped inspire Darwin's theory of evolution.

- The Appalachian Mountains in North America are one of the world's oldest mountain ranges, estimated to be over 480 million years old.

- South Africa is one of the few countries with three capital cities, each serving different branches of government.

- Europe's Blue Lagoon in Iceland is a geothermal spa with warm, mineral-rich waters believed to have healing properties.

- The Southern Ocean, recognized by some as the fifth ocean, surrounds Antarctica and plays a crucial role in Earth's climate system.

- Asia's Mekong River supports the livelihoods of millions through its rich fisheries and fertile floodplains.

- Australia's Great Dividing Range is the third longest land-based mountain range, stretching 2,300 miles.

- Europe's Stonehenge is a prehistoric monument that remains a mystery regarding its construction and purpose.

- North America's Death Valley is one of the hottest places on Earth, with temperatures reaching over 130°F.

- Africa's Namib Desert is one of the world's oldest deserts, with some dunes over 1,000 feet tall.

- South America's Atacama Desert is the driest non-polar desert on Earth, with regions that have never recorded rainfall.

- The Victoria Falls in Africa, known as "The Smoke That Thunders," is the world's largest waterfall by total width and height.

- Asia's Yangtze River is the longest river in the continent and the third-longest in the world.

- Europe's Leaning Tower of Pisa was unintentionally built on unstable soil, causing its famous tilt.

- Australia's Great Ocean Road is one of the world's most scenic coastal drives, passing iconic landmarks like the Twelve Apostles.

- The Okavango Delta in Africa floods seasonally, transforming from a dry savanna to a lush oasis full of wildlife.

- Europe's Scandinavian Peninsula includes some of the world's highest standards of living and quality of life.

- The Great Wall of China, visible from space, is over 13,000 miles long and was built over several dynasties.

- The Rock of Gibraltar in Europe is known for its Barbary macaques, the only wild monkey population in Europe.

- Mount Elbrus, a dormant volcano in Russia, is the highest peak in Europe at 18,510 feet.

- The Great Victoria Desert is the largest desert in Australia, covering an area larger than the United Kingdom.

- North America's Yellowstone National Park contains over half of the world's geysers.

- Europe's Trans-Siberian Railway is the longest rail line, stretching over 5,700 miles across Russia.

- Africa's Congo Basin is the second-largest rainforest, containing a quarter of the world's tropical forests.

- Asia's Tigris and Euphrates Rivers were vital to the ancient civilizations of Mesopotamia.

- Europe's Mount Etna in Italy is the most active volcano on the continent, with frequent eruptions.

- The Outback in Australia covers most of the country's interior and is home to only 10% of the population.

- Lake Titicaca, located between Peru and Bolivia, is the highest navigable lake in the world.

- The Channel Tunnel, connecting the UK to France, is the longest underwater tunnel in the world.

- The Gobi Desert, which spans Mongolia and China, has extreme temperature variations, ranging from -40°F to 122°F.

Awesome History Facts

- The Great Pyramid of Giza was built around 4,500 years ago and was the tallest man-made structure in the world for over 3,800 years.

- The Library of Alexandria, one of the ancient world's largest libraries, was destroyed in a series of incidents, leading to the loss of countless texts.

- Leonardo da Vinci, the Renaissance polymath, wrote backward in his notebooks, using mirror writing likely to keep his ideas private.

- The "Black Death" of the 14th century killed an estimated 25 million people in Europe, reducing the population by nearly a third.

- The shortest war in history was between Britain and the Sultanate of Zanzibar, lasting just 38 minutes in 1896.

- The Mongol Empire, led by Genghis Khan, was the largest contiguous land empire in history, covering over 9 million square miles at its height.

- The Rosetta Stone, discovered in 1799, helped linguists decipher ancient Egyptian hieroglyphics due to its tri-lingual inscription.

- The French Revolution transformed France from a monarchy to a republic and laid the foundation for modern democracy.

- The world's oldest known city, Jericho, in the Country of Palestine, has been continuously inhabited for over 11,000 years.

- The Mayan civilization had an advanced calendar system and a complex writing script but mysteriously collapsed around the 9th century CE.

- The first recorded Olympic Games took place in 776 BCE in Olympia, Greece, with only one event: a footrace.

- The Roman Colosseum could hold up to 50,000 spectators and hosted gladiator contests, animal hunts, and naval battles.

- In ancient Rome, purple was a color reserved for the elite because the dye was expensive and made from a type of sea snail.

- The Hundred Years' War between England and France actually lasted 116 years, from 1337 to 1453.

- The Magna Carta, signed in 1215, was the first document to limit the powers of the English monarchy and laid the groundwork for modern democracy.

- The Berlin Wall separated East and West Berlin from 1961 to 1989, symbolizing the divide between the capitalist West and communist East.

- The Aztec Empire flourished in central Mexico before being conquered by Spanish conquistadors in the early 16th century.

- Cleopatra VII of Egypt, the last pharaoh of ancient Egypt, could speak at least nine languages and was the first Ptolemaic ruler to speak Egyptian.

- The Great Fire of London in 1666 destroyed much of the city but resulted in improved urban planning and construction.

- The French Revolution led to the rise of Napoleon Bonaparte, who eventually declared himself emperor of France.

- The Vikings, known for their seafaring raids, also established trade routes and settlements across Europe and North America.

- The Code of Hammurabi, one of the earliest written legal codes, was inscribed on a stone stele in ancient Babylon around 1754 BCE.

- The Wright brothers made the first powered airplane flight in 1903, launching the era of modern aviation.

- The medieval samurai of Japan adhered to a strict code of honor known as bushido, emphasizing loyalty, courage, and self-discipline.

- The ancient city of Petra in Jordan was carved into rose-red cliffs by the Nabateans over 2,000 years ago.

- Inca engineers constructed the city of Machu Picchu high in the Andes without the use of mortar, fitting stones so tightly that no mortar was needed.

- The Silk Road was a network of trade routes connecting Asia and Europe, allowing for the exchange of silk, spices, and ideas.

- The Crusades were a series of religious wars launched by European Christians to reclaim Jerusalem and the Holy Land from Muslim control.

- Timbuktu in Mali was a significant center of trade and learning during the Mali Empire, renowned for its ancient manuscripts and Islamic universities.

- The ancient Greek philosopher Socrates was sentenced to death for "corrupting the youth" of Athens and died by drinking hemlock.

- Mansa Musa ruled over the Mali empire in the 14th Century, and his incredible access to gold made him arguably the richest human to have ever lived.

- The ancient Indus Valley civilization had advanced urban planning, with cities like Mohenjo-daro featuring grid layouts and drainage systems.

- The Phoenicians, known for their seafaring skills, are credited with developing one of the first alphabets, which influenced modern writing systems.

- The Opium Wars between Britain and China in the 19th century resulted in the cession of Hong Kong to the British.

- The Sumerians, one of the world's earliest civilizations, invented the wheel, cuneiform writing, and the first known calendar.

- The Emancipation Proclamation, issued by U.S. President Abraham Lincoln in 1863, declared the freedom of slaves in Confederate states.

- The ancient Romans had public bathhouses, aqueducts, and sewage systems, showcasing their advanced engineering.

- The Islamic Golden Age from the 8th to the 14th century was a period of cultural and scientific flourishing in the Muslim world.

- The Great Wall of China, built over several dynasties, was constructed to protect against invasions from northern nomadic tribes.

- The Easter Island statues, known as moai, were carved from volcanic rock by the Rapa Nui people between 1400 and 1650 CE.

- The Age of Exploration in the 15th and 16th centuries saw European explorers like Columbus and Magellan expand their empires across the globe.

- The Neolithic Revolution marked the transition from hunter-gatherer societies to settled agriculture and the rise of the first cities.

- The medieval period, or Middle Ages, was characterized by feudalism, where land was owned by nobles and worked by peasants.

- The Ottoman Empire, which lasted over 600 years, controlled much of southeastern Europe, western Asia, and North Africa.

- The first successful vaccine was developed by Edward Jenner in the late 18th century to prevent smallpox.

- The Kingdom of Kush in ancient Nubia (modern Sudan) rivaled Egypt and even ruled Egypt as the 25th Dynasty.

- The Spanish Inquisition was established in 1478 to maintain Catholic orthodoxy in Spain but became infamous for its brutal persecution.

- The Roswell UFO incident of 1947 led to widespread speculation about alien life, fueling modern conspiracy theories.

- The Dutch East India Company was one of the world's first multinational corporations and dominated global trade in the 17th century.

- The French Revolution gave rise to the Reign of Terror, during which thousands of people were executed by guillotine.

- The Treaty of Versailles, which ended World War I, imposed harsh reparations on Germany, contributing to the rise of World War II.

- The Irish Potato Famine of the 1840s led to a massive wave of Irish immigration to the United States.

- The Marshall Plan, initiated after World War II, helped rebuild Europe and prevent the spread of communism.

- The Great Depression of the 1930s resulted in mass unemployment and poverty following a global stock market crash.

- The United Nations was founded in 1945 to promote peace and prevent future world wars following the devastation of World War II.

- The ancient Egyptian pharaoh Akhenaten attempted to establish monotheism, worshiping the sun god Aten exclusively.

- The Spanish conquistadors brought horses to the Americas, which were adopted by Native American tribes for hunting and warfare.

- The Russian Revolution of 1917 led to the establishment of the Soviet Union under Vladimir Lenin and later Joseph Stalin.

- The Trojan War, described in Homer's "Iliad," is believed to have occurred around the 12th century BCE, though its historicity is debated.

- The Renaissance was a period of renewed interest in classical learning, art, and science that began in Italy in the 14th century.

- The Great Leap Forward, a campaign led by Mao Zedong in China, resulted in widespread famine and the deaths of millions.

- The Protestant Reformation, led by Martin Luther in the 16th century, resulted in the split of Christianity into Catholic and Protestant branches.

- The Manhattan Project during World War II developed the first nuclear weapons, leading to the bombings of Hiroshima and Nagasaki.

- The Code of Justinian, a collection of Roman laws, greatly influenced the development of modern legal systems.

- The Haitian Revolution of 1791-1804 was the only successful slave revolt, leading to the establishment of Haiti as an independent nation.

- The Salem witch trials in 1692 led to the execution of 20 people and marked a dark period of religious hysteria in colonial America.

- The Ancestral Puebloans, also known as the Anasazi, built cliff dwellings in the American Southwest around 1,000 years ago.

- The Berlin Conference of 1884-1885 regulated European colonization of Africa, leading to the "Scramble for Africa."

- The Irish monks preserved many classical texts during the Dark Ages, contributing to the Carolingian Renaissance.

- The sinking of the Titanic in 1912 resulted in the deaths of over 1,500 people and led to improvements in maritime safety.

- The Battle of Stalingrad in World War II was one of the deadliest battles in history, resulting in over a million casualties.

- The Battle of Waterloo in 1815 marked the defeat of Napoleon Bonaparte and ended the Napoleonic Wars.

- The First Opium War between Britain and China ended with the Treaty of Nanking, opening Chinese ports to foreign trade.

- The Knights Templar, a medieval Christian military order, became wealthy and influential before being disbanded in the 14th century.

- The ancient Greeks believed that the Oracle of Delphi could predict the future, and leaders sought its guidance.

- The Manhattan Project during World War II developed the first nuclear weapons, leading to the atomic bombings of Hiroshima and Nagasaki.

- The Sumerians of Mesopotamia, considered one of the world's first civilizations, developed the earliest known writing system called cuneiform.

- The Maya civilization had an advanced calendar system and used sophisticated astronomical observations.

Games and Sports

- The longest tennis match in history took over 11 hours and was played between John Isner and Nicolas Mahut at Wimbledon in 2010.

- The FIFA World Cup trophy was once stolen in 1966 and found a week later by a dog named Pickles in London.

- Golf is one of the few sports played on the moon; astronaut Alan Shepard famously hit two golf balls during the Apollo 14 mission.

- The shortest boxing match on record lasted just 4 seconds after Mike Collins knocked out Pat Brownson with a single punch in 1947.

- The fastest goal ever scored in soccer happened after just 2.4 seconds in 1998 by Nawaf Al Abed in a Saudi league match.

- The Olympic Games were originally a religious festival in ancient Greece, held in honor of Zeus and lasting up to six months.

- In chess, a phenomenon called "The Immortal Game" occurred in 1851, known for its remarkable tactical play by Adolf Anderssen.

- Basketball was invented in 1891 by Dr. James Naismith, who used a peach basket as the original hoop.

- The Tour de France was originally created to promote a newspaper and has since become the world's most famous cycling race.

- Cricket matches between teams of blind players are possible because the ball contains bearings that rattle, allowing players to hear it.

- In ancient Roman chariot races, the teams were so popular that fans would often riot if their team lost.

- The longest baseball game lasted 33 innings over eight hours and 25 minutes between the Rochester Red Wings and Pawtucket Red Sox in 1981.

- In curling, players vigorously sweep the ice to reduce friction and control the stone's direction and distance.

- The first Super Bowl was held in 1967 between the NFL's Green Bay Packers and AFL's Kansas City Chiefs.

- In ancient Chinese cuju, an early form of soccer, soldiers kicked leather balls into a small net.

- The 1921-1922 cricket season in Australia saw 903 runs scored in one day, a record that still stands.

- Formula One drivers experience g-forces greater than astronauts do during liftoff due to the high speeds and quick turns.

- Lacrosse is the oldest team sport in North America, originating with the Iroquois and other Indigenous peoples before European contact.

- The heaviest sumo wrestler ever recorded, Yamamotoyama Ryūta, weighed over 600 pounds at his peak.

- Table tennis was banned in the Soviet Union from 1930 to 1950 because authorities thought it was harmful to players' eyes.

- The world record for holding one's breath underwater is over 24 minutes, set by Aleix Segura in 2016.

- The first recorded reference to baseball is from 1744 in England, while the sport was popularized in the U.S. in the 19th century.

- Some professional chess players burn up to 6,000 calories a day during tournaments due to the intense mental concentration.

- The FIFA World Cup is the most-watched sporting event globally, with more than 3.5 billion viewers in 2018.

- Tug-of-war was an Olympic sport from 1900 to 1920, with teams of five pulling on opposite ends of a rope.

- In kabaddi, a popular sport in South Asia, a player must tag opponents while holding their breath and chanting "kabaddi."

- Skateboarding was banned in Norway from 1978 to 1989 due to safety concerns.

- In the Eton Wall Game, a peculiar form of football, players attempt to move the ball along a narrow field by the wall.

- The marathon's 26.2-mile distance was standardized in the 1908 Olympics to accommodate the British royal family.

- The world's longest marathon tennis rally lasted 50,970 strokes and was played over 14 hours in 2017.

- The only person to win Olympic medals in both the Winter and Summer Games was Eddie Eagan, winning gold in boxing and bobsleigh.

- In rugby, a "try" was originally not worth any points and only earned the opportunity to "try" to kick for a goal.

- Badminton players smash shuttlecocks at speeds exceeding 200 mph, making it one of the fastest sports.

- Gymnastics is rooted in ancient Greek exercises intended to prepare young men for war.

- The highest score ever recorded in a single basketball game was 100 points by Wilt Chamberlain in 1962.

- In fencing, the first known fencing manual dates back to the 14th century, outlining techniques for European sword fighting.

- The most common way to determine the outcome of a baseball game that is tied after nine innings is extra innings, but in Japan's Nippon Professional Baseball, games can end in a tie.

- In Australian rules football, players can use any part of their body to move the ball and score by kicking it through goalposts.

- Modern pentathlon is based on the skills required of a 19th-century soldier: shooting, fencing, swimming, horse riding, and running.

- Jai alai, popular in Spain, is played with a curved basket glove called a "cesta" to catch and hurl the ball at speeds up to 188 mph.

- In hockey, the original pucks were frozen cow dung, which eventually gave way to rubber and other materials.

- The NFL's Detroit Lions and Dallas Cowboys have hosted Thanksgiving Day games almost every year since the 1930s.

- Korfball, similar to basketball but invented in the Netherlands, requires teams to have both male and female players.

- In competitive eating, Joey Chestnut set a record by eating 76 hot dogs in 10 minutes during the 2021 Nathan's Hot Dog Eating Contest.

- The world's largest chess set is located in St. Louis, Missouri, with pieces nearly 6 feet tall.

- Snooker players often apply chalk to their cue tips to increase friction and improve control when striking the ball.

- In modern football (soccer), players run an average of 7 miles per game.

- The world's longest recorded cricket match lasted 10 days between England and South Africa in 1939 but ended in a draw due to England's travel schedule.

- The term "hat trick" in hockey originated in cricket, where players were awarded hats for taking three wickets in a row.

- Polo is one of the oldest team sports, originating over 2,000 years ago in Persia and played on horseback.

Popular Myths and Mysterious Artifacts

- The Loch Ness Monster, or "Nessie," is a legendary creature reportedly living in Loch Ness, with sightings dating back to the 6th century.

- The Phaistos Disc is a clay tablet from ancient Crete containing unknown symbols that have confounded linguists since its discovery.

- In Filipino folklore, the aswang is a shape-shifting creature that turns into a monster at night but appears human during the day.

- The Georgia Guidestones, erected in 1980, have inscriptions that outline principles for humanity's future, written in several languages.

- In Norse mythology, Yggdrasil, the World Tree, connects the nine realms and serves as the axis of the universe.

- The Voynich Manuscript is a mysterious medieval book written in an undeciphered language with strange illustrations.

- The Phoenix is a mythical bird that burns itself to ashes upon death and is reborn, representing renewal and immortality.

- The city of Atlantis, first mentioned by Plato, is thought to be fictional, yet some explorers still search for its location.

- The Dogon tribe in Mali knew about the star Sirius B before telescopes could discover it, which has puzzled researchers.

- The Oracle of Delphi, an ancient Greek priestess, inhaled gases to have visions and deliver prophecies to visitors.

- The Nazino Affair in Soviet Russia resulted in settlers being sent to an island and eventually resorting to cannibalism due to starvation.

- The Antikythera Mechanism, an ancient Greek device discovered in a shipwreck, is believed to have tracked celestial movements like an early computer.

- The Moai statues of Easter Island remain an architectural mystery due to their size and the means by which they were transported and erected.

- The Coral Castle in Florida was built singlehandedly by Edward Leedskalnin using giant stones, but he never disclosed his methods.

- The chupacabra, a creature in Latin American folklore, drinks the blood of livestock and is often described as reptilian.

- The Taos Hum is a low-frequency sound reported by residents of Taos, New Mexico, but its source remains unidentified despite research.

- The Kraken, a colossal sea monster from Norse mythology, supposedly terrorized sailors and pulled ships to their doom.

- In Hindu mythology, Hanuman, the monkey god, is a symbol of strength and devotion and features prominently in the epic "Ramayana."

- The Minotaur, a half-bull monster in Greek mythology, was imprisoned in a labyrinth and ultimately slain by Theseus.

- The Headless Horseman, from Washington Irving's "The Legend of Sleepy Hollow," is based on an old European ghost story.

- The Cailleach, a hag in Scottish and Irish mythology, controls the weather and is associated with winter.

- The Green Children of Woolpit were two children who appeared in an English village in the 12th century speaking an unknown language.

- The Dancing Plague of 1518 saw hundreds of people in Strasbourg dance non-stop for weeks, leading to exhaustion and death.

- The Codex Gigas, or Devil's Bible, is a medieval manuscript with a full-page illustration of the devil and is said to have been written in a single night.

- King Arthur's legendary sword, Excalibur, was either pulled from a stone or given to him by the Lady of the Lake, depending on the version of the legend.

- In Japanese folklore, kitsune (fox spirits) are believed to possess humans, shape-shift into beautiful women, or bring fortune.

- The Mary Celeste, an American merchant ship, was found adrift in the Atlantic in 1872 with no crew, despite being fully stocked with supplies.

- The Lady in White is a ghostly figure common in folklore across cultures, often linked to tragic love stories or betrayal.

- The Loretto Chapel staircase in Santa Fe has no visible support and is said to have been built by a mysterious carpenter.

- The Bermuda Triangle is a region in the Atlantic Ocean infamous for the unexplained disappearances of ships and planes over the years.

- Stonehenge, an ancient stone circle in England, is an enigma in terms of its construction and the people who built it.

- The Wendigo, a creature from Algonquian folklore, represents insatiable greed and hunger and preys on humans who succumb to their desires.

- The Tulli Papyrus, an ancient Egyptian document, supposedly describes strange flying objects, leading to theories about early UFO sightings.

- Baba Yaga, a witch in Slavic folklore, lives in a house on chicken legs and flies in a mortar and pestle.

- The Sphinx, a mythical creature with the head of a woman, body of a lion, and wings of a bird, posed riddles to travelers in Greek legend.

- The Oak Island Money Pit is a mysterious shaft that supposedly holds buried treasure, but no one has reached the bottom.

- The Ulfberht swords, high-quality Viking blades, contain steel so advanced that historians are unsure of its origin.

- The Jersey Devil, said to roam the Pine Barrens of New Jersey, is often described with hooves, wings, and a horse-like head.

- The Yeti, or Abominable Snowman, is believed to inhabit the Himalayas and has been part of local folklore for centuries.

- Elves in Icelandic folklore are thought to live in rocks and hills, and it's considered bad luck to disturb their homes.

Economics and Currency

- The "Big Mac Index," created by The Economist, uses the price of a Big Mac burger as a measure of purchasing power parity across countries.

- Zimbabwe experienced one of the worst hyperinflations in history in the late 2000s, with prices doubling daily at its peak, leading to the issuance of a 100 trillion-dollar banknote.

- The U.S. dollar is the most widely used currency in the world, with more than 60% of all global currency reserves held in dollars.

- The Yapese people of Micronesia used giant stone discs called Rai stones as currency, some measuring up to 12 feet in diameter.

- Tulipmania in 17th-century Holland was one of the first recorded speculative bubbles, where tulip bulb prices skyrocketed before collapsing.

- The Bitcoin network uses more electricity than some small countries due to the computational power required for mining.

- During World War II, some Allied prisoners in German POW camps used Monopoly money sent in care packages to buy their way out.

- The global economy shrank by over 15% during the Great Depression, a period of widespread unemployment and poverty in the 1930s.

- The largest U.S. banknote ever printed was the $100,000 gold certificate, used exclusively for transactions between Federal Reserve Banks.

- In ancient Rome, soldiers were sometimes paid in salt, giving rise to the word "salary," which is derived from the Latin word "salarium."

- The Bank of England, established in 1694, is one of the world's oldest central banks and initially began as a private institution.

- The Bretton Woods Conference in 1944 established the International Monetary Fund (IMF) and World Bank, shaping global finance after WWII.

- During the 2008 financial crisis, Lehman Brothers filed for the largest bankruptcy in history, with debts of over $600 billion.

- Sweden is rapidly moving toward becoming a cashless society, with over 80% of transactions now conducted electronically.

- In Venezuela, hyperinflation forced the government to remove five zeros from its currency in 2018, rendering banknotes nearly worthless.

- Ancient Mesopotamians are believed to have invented the first forms of writing to record economic transactions over 5,000 years ago.

- The world's oldest known coin, the Lydian stater, was made from electrum and used in the kingdom of Lydia (modern-day Turkey) around 600 BCE.

- Some of the first paper money was used in China over 1,000 years ago during the Tang and Song dynasties.

- The "Nixon shock" in 1971 ended the U.S. dollar's convertibility to gold, effectively ending the Bretton Woods system and creating the modern floating exchange rate.

- "Laissez-faire" economics advocates for minimal government intervention in markets, a concept famously championed by economist Adam Smith.

- The Swiss franc is considered one of the world's most stable currencies, often serving as a "safe haven" in times of economic turmoil.

- Cigarettes were used as a form of currency in Germany following World War II due to the scarcity of other commodities.

Plants and Insects

- Bamboo is the fastest-growing plant in the world, with some species able to grow up to 35 inches in just one day.

- The Venus flytrap snaps shut on unsuspecting insects in less than a second, using its sensitive hairs to detect prey.

- The giant water lily's leaves can grow over 10 feet wide and are strong enough to support a small child.

- Dung beetles can roll balls of dung 1,100 times their own weight back to their burrows, which is like a human lifting an elephant.

- Fireflies, or lightning bugs, create their magical glow using special organs that produce light without heat.

- The praying mantis sometimes sways like a leaf to blend in with the plants and sneak up on its insect prey.

- Monarch butterflies travel up to 3,000 miles every year to find warmer weather in Mexico and avoid cold winters.

- Leafcutter ants are tiny farmers who grow fungus in their nests using leaves they collect, creating miniature farms underground.

- The titan beetle is one of the largest insects, reaching up to 6.6 inches long with mandibles strong enough to snap a pencil.

- Cicadas spend most of their lives underground before emerging every 13 or 17 years to sing and lay eggs.

- Dragonflies can zip around at speeds up to 35 mph and can fly backward, forward, and sideways like a helicopter.

- The waterwheel plant, a cousin of the Venus flytrap, captures tiny aquatic creatures in its underwater traps.

- Army ants work together to form bridges using their bodies, allowing them to cross streams and gaps.

- The bladderwort is a carnivorous plant with tiny bladders that suck in small water bugs when triggered.

- Pitcher plants look like tall pitchers full of water, but they use sweet nectar to trap insects inside.

- Giant redwoods can grow over 300 feet tall, making them the tallest trees on Earth and providing homes for many animals.

- The atlas moth is one of the largest insects, with a wingspan of nearly a foot, and its wings look like snake heads.

- Bumblebees can "buzz pollinate" flowers by vibrating their wings, which helps loosen the pollen.

- The corpse flower's giant bloom gives off a strong smell like rotting meat, which attracts flies to help with pollination.

- Green lacewings release a stinky smell to scare away predators, and their larvae use debris to hide themselves.

- Some ants care for aphids like farmers, protecting them in exchange for the sweet honeydew they produce.

- The leaf-mimic katydid has wings that look exactly like leaves, allowing it to hide perfectly from predators.

- The golden poison dart frog gets its toxic skin from eating poisonous insects, but it's harmless in captivity.

- The Brazilian treehopper looks strange with its horn-like protrusion covered in what looks like extra antennae.

- The sundew is a carnivorous plant with sticky tentacles that trap insects, which are then slowly digested.

- The hickory horned devil caterpillar may look fierce with its spiky horns, but it's completely harmless to humans.

- Army ants can even make protective tents out of their bodies, providing shade for the queen and their young.

- The titan arum's massive bloom can grow over 10 feet tall and smells like rotten fish to attract pollinators.

- Pea aphids can produce their own colorful pigments like plants, making them one of the few animals to do so.

- Oak trees produce different amounts of acorns each year to trick animals into not eating all of their seeds.

Fashion and Clothing

- High heels were originally worn by men in the 17th century, particularly by the French aristocracy, before becoming fashionable for women.

- Jeans were invented by Jacob Davis and Levi Strauss in 1873 as sturdy work pants for miners during the California Gold Rush.

- The first fashion magazine, "Journal des Dames et des Modes," was published in France in 1797 and helped spread trends across Europe.

- In Victorian England, women wore "crinolines," large hoop skirts supported by steel frames that sometimes caused injuries and accidents.

- The kimono, a traditional Japanese garment, dates back over 1,000 years and is worn for different occasions based on the pattern and fabric.

- The term "haute couture," or high fashion, originated in Paris and is legally protected, only applying to fashion houses that meet strict criteria.

- In the Middle Ages, sumptuary laws dictated who could wear certain colors or fabrics based on social rank, often limiting purple to royalty.

- During World War II, women drew lines on their legs with eyeliner to mimic stockings, which were rationed due to nylon shortages.

- The modern-day necktie evolved from the cravat, a piece of cloth worn by Croatian mercenaries in the 17th century.

- In the 19th century, the bicycle craze prompted women to adopt "bloomers," an early form of pants that were more practical for cycling.

- Zippers, invented in 1893, became popular in fashion after being marketed as a practical replacement for buttons and hooks.

- The color "Prussian blue" was a significant discovery in the early 18th century, marking the first modern synthetic pigment used in textiles.

- The tuxedo, named after Tuxedo Park, New York, was introduced in the late 19th century as a more casual alternative to tailcoats.

- In the 1970s, platform shoes became a fashion staple, with some reaching over 6 inches in height and embraced by musicians like David Bowie.

- The trench coat was designed by Thomas Burberry during World War I as a lightweight, waterproof coat for British soldiers.

Famous Hoaxes and Conspiracies

- Bigfoot, or Sasquatch, is a cryptid often described as a giant ape-man in North American forests, but many of the sightings and footprints have been revealed as hoaxes.

- The Piltdown Man, a fossil discovery in 1912, was once believed to be the "missing link" between apes and humans but was later exposed as a forgery created by combining human and orangutan bones.

- The Protocols of the Elders of Zion is a fabricated anti-Semitic text that falsely claims to reveal a Jewish plot for world domination, used to incite hatred and violence in the 20th century.

- The Cardiff Giant, supposedly a petrified prehistoric man, was actually a gypsum statue buried as a prank in New York state and uncovered in 1869 to much public excitement.

- The War of the Worlds radio broadcast by Orson Welles in 1938 caused widespread panic as listeners believed that Martians were invading New Jersey, despite repeated disclaimers that it was fiction.

- The Cottingley Fairies were photographs taken by two young girls in 1917, supposedly showing real fairies, but later admitted to be cutout drawings.

- The Bermuda Triangle is believed to be a region where ships and planes mysteriously vanish, but investigations have shown that these incidents are no more frequent than in other heavily traveled regions.

- The moon landing conspiracy claims that the Apollo missions to the moon were staged, often citing misinterpreted photographic evidence, despite overwhelming proof of NASA's achievement.

- The Loch Ness Monster is believed to inhabit Scotland's Loch Ness, but the most famous photograph of the creature, taken in 1934, was later revealed to be a staged hoax.

- The Hitler Diaries, allegedly personal diaries of Adolf Hitler, were revealed to be a forgery when analyzed by experts in 1983.

- Crop circles, often attributed to extraterrestrials, were confessed to be created by two British pranksters in the 1970s, sparking global trends of crop circle-making.

- The "Paul is Dead" conspiracy claimed that Paul McCartney of The Beatles had died and was replaced by a lookalike, fueled by supposed clues in their album covers and songs.

- The Flat Earth Society, despite centuries of scientific evidence proving Earth is round, continues to believe that Earth is a flat disc.

- The Majestic-12 conspiracy claims that the U.S. government formed a secret committee to investigate UFOs, but the documents supporting the theory have been widely discredited.

- The Diatlov Pass incident, where nine hikers died in the Ural Mountains in 1959 under mysterious circumstances, has sparked theories involving UFOs, yetis, and secret military experiments.

- The Hollow Earth theory suggests that the Earth is hollow and inhabited by advanced civilizations or creatures, with some proponents claiming that secret entrances exist at the poles.

- Project MKUltra was a secret CIA program that experimented with mind control and LSD, which later led to many conspiracy theories after its partial declassification.

- The Philadelphia Experiment, a supposed U.S. Navy project in 1943, is claimed to have teleported a ship through space and time, but no credible evidence supports this.

- The New Coke conspiracy theory holds that Coca-Cola intentionally released a poor-tasting "New Coke" formula to boost sales of Classic Coke.

- Operation Northwoods was a proposed false-flag operation involving fake attacks to justify U.S. military intervention in Cuba, but it was never executed.

- The Denver International Airport is rumored to contain secret underground bunkers and unusual murals, fueling conspiracy theories about a global elite.

- The CIA has been accused of orchestrating the assassination of John F. Kennedy, with conflicting evidence leading to countless theories on his death.

- The Bilderberg Group, an annual meeting of political and business leaders, is often accused of conspiring to control global politics and economies.

- The "Chemtrails" conspiracy theory posits that contrails from airplanes contain chemical agents deliberately sprayed for unknown purposes.

- The Vatican Secret Archives, a collection of confidential documents, is rumored to contain secret prophecies and suppressed knowledge.

- The 5G conspiracy theory claims that 5G cellular networks cause illnesses, despite scientific evidence debunking such links.

- Operation Gladio was a secret NATO program to counter potential Soviet invasions, but its existence has led to theories about ongoing covert operations in Europe.

Military History and Warfare

- The Battle of Marathon in 490 BCE was a pivotal victory for the Greeks against Persia and inspired the modern marathon race, allegedly based on a soldier's 26-mile run to Athens.

- Hannibal famously crossed the Alps with war elephants during the Second Punic War to surprise the Romans, achieving significant victories in Italy.

- The Great Wall of China was originally built to protect against northern invasions but was only moderately successful, as it couldn't stop all attackers.

- The medieval knight's armor was so heavy that knights often needed assistance to mount their horses and could drown if they fell into water.

- The Mongol Empire created one of the largest and most efficient communication networks in the world, known as the Yam, to transmit messages quickly across vast distances.

- Napoleon Bonaparte was known for his innovative battlefield tactics, often using speed and deception to outmaneuver larger enemies.

- The Battle of Hastings in 1066, where William the Conqueror defeated King Harold, was the last successful invasion of England.

- During the American Civil War, the USS Monitor and CSS Virginia (Merrimack) were the first ironclad warships to engage in naval combat, changing naval warfare forever.

- Trench warfare during World War I resulted in a brutal stalemate on the Western Front, with soldiers living in terrible conditions and often gaining only a few yards of ground.

- The Spanish Armada, intended to invade England in 1588, was crippled by smaller English ships and severe weather, resulting in a devastating defeat for Spain.

- The blitzkrieg tactics used by Germany during World War II emphasized rapid movement of tanks and aircraft, overwhelming enemies before they could respond.

- In the Battle of Stalingrad during World War II, intense fighting left nearly 2 million dead and marked a turning point against Nazi Germany.

- The Trojan Horse, described in Greek mythology, was a large wooden horse left as a gift to Troy but contained Greek soldiers who opened the city gates for the invading army.

- The ancient Greek phalanx formation was highly effective in battle, with rows of soldiers protecting each other using long spears and overlapping shields.

- Sun Tzu's "The Art of War," written over 2,000 years ago, remains one of the most influential military strategy texts and is still studied today.

- The "scorched earth" policy, where armies destroy resources to prevent enemies from using them, was famously used by Russia during Napoleon's invasion.

- The Siege of Leningrad lasted nearly 900 days during World War II, resulting in the deaths of over a million civilians due to starvation and bombardment.

- The Inca Empire used a system of knotted strings called quipus to record military information and logistics across their vast territory.

- The Cold War was marked by an arms race between the United States and the Soviet Union, leading to massive stockpiles of nuclear weapons but no direct conflict.

- Hannibal's tactical genius was evident at the Battle of Cannae, where his forces encircled and annihilated a much larger Roman army.

- The Zulu warriors of southern Africa were known for their discipline and innovative tactics, particularly their "horns of the buffalo" formation.

- The longest siege in history was the Siege of Candia (now Heraklion) on Crete, lasting 21 years (1648-1669) between Venetian and Ottoman forces.

- The "Enigma" machine used by Nazi Germany was eventually cracked by Allied codebreakers, helping them intercept and decode critical messages.

- The Doolittle Raid in World War II was a daring bombing mission on Tokyo by U.S. forces, demonstrating Japan's vulnerability after Pearl Harbor.

- The Battle of the Somme in World War I saw the first use of tanks in combat, marking the beginning of mechanized warfare.

- The ancient Assyrians are considered one of the first to establish a professional standing army, which dominated the Middle East.

- The use of carrier pigeons for military communication dates back to ancient times and was common up through World War I.

- The Battle of Thermopylae, fought by King Leonidas and his 300 Spartans, was a heroic defense against the much larger Persian army.

- The Cuban Missile Crisis of 1962 brought the U.S. and Soviet Union to the brink of nuclear war, narrowly avoiding a catastrophe through diplomatic negotiations.

Prison and Crime

- In 1962, three inmates (Frank Morris and brothers John and Clarence Anglin) escaped from Alcatraz, the notorious "escape-proof" prison, using a makeshift raft and leaving behind dummy heads in their beds. Their fate remains a mystery.

- In 1945, over 600 prisoners and guards escaped from Stalag Luft III, a German POW camp, in an event known as "The Great Escape." However, many were recaptured or killed after the breakout.

- The Maze Prison escape in 1983 saw 38 IRA prisoners use smuggled guns to overpower guards and flee the maximum-security prison in Northern Ireland.

- El Chapo, the Mexican drug lord, famously escaped from a high-security prison in 2015 through a mile-long tunnel complete with lighting and ventilation, dug from his cell.

- The Texas Seven were a group of seven inmates who broke out of a Texas prison in 2000, remaining on the run for over a month before being captured.

- The Libby Prison escape in 1864 saw over 100 Union soldiers tunnel their way out of the Confederate-run facility in Richmond, Virginia.

- In 2001, two convicted killers escaped from King County Jail in Seattle by removing the toilet in their cell and crawling through the walls to freedom.

- Pascal Payet, a French criminal, escaped prison three times using helicopters hijacked by accomplices, becoming known for his daring aerial breakouts.

- The Dannemora prison escape of 2015 involved two inmates, Richard Matt and David Sweat, using tools to cut through steel walls and pipes, but they were eventually recaptured after a weeks-long manhunt.

- In 1998, four inmates used a smuggled cell phone to orchestrate an escape from a Brazilian prison, having accomplices rent a house nearby and tunnel under the prison walls.

- The 1971 Attica Prison riot in New York resulted in one of the largest prison takeovers, with inmates holding 42 guards hostage for four days before authorities stormed the facility.

- In 2009, two inmates used hacksaw blades to escape from the Curran-Fromhold Correctional Facility in Philadelphia by cutting through bars and climbing down a rope made of bed sheets.

- The French outlaw Jacques Mesrine was known for escaping from prison multiple times, once even taking a judge hostage during an attempt.

- The largest heist in history was the $1 billion looted from Iraq's Central Bank in 2003, reportedly on orders from Saddam Hussein shortly before the Iraq War.

- In the late 1970s, the United States experienced a surge of serial killers, including Ted Bundy, John Wayne Gacy, and the Son of Sam, leaving the country in fear.

- The Great Train Robbery of 1963 involved a gang of 15 thieves who stole £2.6 million from a Royal Mail train in England, equivalent to around £50 million today.

- The Isabella Stewart Gardner Museum heist in Boston in 1990 saw thieves dressed as police officers steal 13 pieces of art valued at over $500 million.

- "Operation Underworld" during World War II was a collaboration between the U.S. Navy and the Mafia to prevent Axis sabotage at New York ports.

- The Hatton Garden heist in London (2015) involved elderly thieves using diamond drills to break into a vault, stealing nearly £14 million in jewelry and cash.

- The "Unabomber," Ted Kaczynski, eluded capture for over 17 years while mailing homemade bombs to scientists and academics, killing three and injuring 23.

- The 1997 North Hollywood shootout involved two bank robbers armed with assault rifles and body armor, resulting in a 44-minute gun battle with the LAPD.

- The infamous pirate Blackbeard (Edward Teach) captured a French slave ship and turned it into his flagship, the Queen Anne's Revenge.

- The Saint Valentine's Day Massacre in 1929 saw seven members of Chicago's North Side Gang killed, allegedly on orders from Al Capone.

- The Green River Killer, Gary Ridgway, was one of the most prolific serial killers in U.S. history, confessing to murdering at least 49 women over 20 years.

- Pablo Escobar, the infamous Colombian drug lord, was so wealthy that he spent thousands of dollars annually on rubber bands to bundle his cash.

- The Ponzi scheme, named after Charles Ponzi, defrauded investors in the 1920s by promising high returns from investments that didn't exist.

- The Brinks Job in Boston (1950) saw thieves steal nearly $3 million from an armored car depot, considered "the crime of the century" at the time.

- Frank Abagnale, a master con artist and the subject of "Catch Me If You Can," posed as a pilot, doctor, and lawyer while cashing over $2.5 million in fraudulent checks.

- The French Connection was a heroin-smuggling operation in the 1960s that used transatlantic routes to transport drugs from Turkey through France to the U.S.

- In 1971, D.B. Cooper hijacked a plane and demanded $200,000 before parachuting out and vanishing, leading to one of the FBI's longest unsolved cases.

- The Boston Strangler terrorized the city in the 1960s, murdering 13 women before Albert DeSalvo confessed, although doubts persist about his guilt.

- The Lindbergh kidnapping in 1932 saw the infant son of aviator Charles Lindbergh kidnapped from his nursery and found dead weeks later.

- The Lufthansa heist in 1978, as dramatized in the movie "Goodfellas," was the largest cash robbery on American soil at the time, with around $5 million stolen.

- The "Pizza Bomber" case involved a complex bank robbery where the perpetrator strapped a bomb to a pizza delivery driver, who was then forced to rob a bank.

- The Zodiac Killer taunted police with cryptic letters in California during the late 1960s but was never apprehended, and his true identity remains unknown.

- Bernie Madoff ran the largest Ponzi scheme in history, defrauding investors out of an estimated $64.8 billion over several decades.

Movies and Cinema

- "Titanic" (1997) was so expensive to produce that it almost bankrupted 20th Century Fox, but its success made it the first film to gross over $1 billion.

- "Star Wars" (1977) was rejected by multiple studios before being picked up by 20th Century Fox, where it became a cultural phenomenon and launched one of the most successful franchises.

- The shark animatronics used in "Jaws" (1975) malfunctioned so frequently that director Steven Spielberg had to rely on music and camera techniques to imply the shark's presence, which heightened the suspense.

- "The Wizard of Oz" (1939) initially featured a silver slipper but was changed to ruby slippers to take advantage of the Technicolor process.

- "Psycho" (1960) caused such a stir that Alfred Hitchcock demanded no one be admitted into the theater after the movie started.

- "The Godfather" (1972) faced challenges with the real-life Mafia, which tried to stop the production but eventually agreed not to interfere if the word "Mafia" wasn't used in the film.

- "The Matrix" (1999) used an innovative "bullet time" camera effect that involved over 100 still cameras to create 360-degree slow-motion scenes.

- "Gone with the Wind" (1939) used over 1,400 extras for the famous scene where injured Confederate soldiers lie sprawled across a train depot.

- "Jurassic Park" (1993) was one of the first major films to blend CGI and practical effects, making its dinosaurs incredibly realistic for its time.

- In "The Dark Knight" (2008), Heath Ledger stayed in character as the Joker for the entire shoot and improvised many of his lines.

- "Pulp Fiction" (1994) revived John Travolta's career and turned Quentin Tarantino into a household name with its nonlinear storytelling.

- "Avatar" (2009) used motion capture extensively to animate the Na'vi, allowing actors to perform in a virtual world in real time.

- In "The Silence of the Lambs" (1991), Anthony Hopkins only appeared on screen for about 16 minutes, yet won the Oscar for Best Actor.

- "Rocky" (1976) was shot in 28 days on a budget of under $1 million, with Sylvester Stallone writing the script in three days.

- "Forrest Gump" (1994) featured groundbreaking visual effects, seamlessly integrating Tom Hanks into historical footage with real-life figures.

- "Inception" (2010) was originally envisioned as a horror film but evolved into a sci-fi thriller about dreams.

- "Schindler's List" (1993) was shot almost entirely in black and white, except for a red coat worn by a little girl as a poignant visual.

- "Back to the Future" (1985) initially cast Eric Stoltz as Marty McFly but replaced him with Michael J. Fox after a few weeks of filming.

- "Toy Story" (1995) was the first entirely computer-animated feature film, leading to the rise of modern CGI-animated movies.

- "A Clockwork Orange" (1971) was banned in the UK for nearly three decades due to its graphic violence, but it remained available in the U.S.

- "E.T. the Extra-Terrestrial" (1982) used Reese's Pieces to lure E.T. instead of M&M's because the latter declined an offer for product placement.

- "The Blair Witch Project" (1999) was shot in just eight days on a $60,000 budget and grossed nearly $250 million worldwide, popularizing the "found footage" genre.

- "Casablanca" (1942) featured rewritten lines even as filming progressed, with the famous "Here's looking at you, kid" line improvised by Humphrey Bogart.

- "Indiana Jones and the Temple of Doom" (1984) led to the creation of the PG-13 rating after parents complained it was too intense for a PG rating.

- "2001: A Space Odyssey" (1968) used a giant rotating set to film zero-gravity scenes, a pioneering technique for its time.

- "Braveheart" (1995) won five Oscars despite historical inaccuracies, inspiring renewed interest in medieval Scotland.

- "Mad Max: Fury Road" (2015) filmed over 90% of its action scenes using practical effects rather than CGI, adding to the film's realism.

- "Alien" (1979) terrified audiences with its groundbreaking "chestburster" scene, which was kept secret from the actors to capture genuine reactions.

- "Goodfellas" (1990) featured a one-take tracking shot through a nightclub kitchen, which took seven hours to rehearse and eight attempts to film.

- "The Lord of the Rings" trilogy (2001-2003) was shot back-to-back over 18 months in New Zealand, with each film featuring over 1,000 special effects shots.

- "Avengers: Endgame" (2019) broke the record for the highest-grossing film of all time, earning over $2.8 billion worldwide and dethroning "Avatar."

- In "Mad Max: Fury Road" (2015), director George Miller used minimal CGI, relying heavily on practical stunts and effects to create the film's intense action scenes.

- "Inception" (2010) was originally envisioned as a horror film before evolving into a heist thriller about shared dreams, with Christopher Nolan directing a 10-hour shooting schedule.

- "Frozen" (2013) became the highest-grossing animated film of its time, with the song "Let It Go" becoming a cultural phenomenon and winning an Academy Award.

- "Get Out" (2017), Jordan Peele's directorial debut, received universal acclaim and was praised for its sharp social commentary on racism.

- "Parasite" (2019) made history as the first non-English-language film to win the Academy Award for Best Picture.

- "Spider-Man: Into the Spider-Verse" (2018) used a groundbreaking animation style, blending CGI with hand-drawn techniques to give it a comic book look.

- "Dunkirk" (2017), directed by Christopher Nolan, was shot using IMAX cameras to capture the epic scale of the World War II evacuation.

- "Interstellar" (2014) featured scientifically accurate depictions of wormholes and black holes, with guidance from physicist Kip Thorne.

- "The Irishman" (2019) employed digital de-aging technology to make its stars appear younger, enabling Robert De Niro to play his character over multiple decades.

- "The Shape of Water" (2017), directed by Guillermo del Toro, featured a mute protagonist and a creature that took nearly three hours to apply prosthetics and makeup to each day.

- "Joker" (2019), a dark origin story, became the highest-grossing R-rated film of all time, grossing over $1 billion worldwide.

- "La La Land" (2016) was initially supposed to have Miles Teller and Emma Watson in the lead roles, but casting changes led to Ryan Gosling and Emma Stone.

- "Black Panther" (2018) became the first superhero film to receive an Academy Award nomination for Best Picture and won three Oscars.

- "Coco" (2017) was inspired by Mexican traditions of the Day of the Dead and featured an all-Latino voice cast.

- "Birdman" (2014) was filmed to appear as if it was shot in one continuous take, creating a seamless visual experience.

- "A Quiet Place" (2018), directed by John Krasinski, relied heavily on sound design and minimal dialogue, adding to its suspenseful atmosphere.

- "Roma" (2018) was shot in black and white and featured non-professional actors to create an authentic depiction of 1970s Mexico.

- "Moana" (2016) enlisted South Pacific cultural experts to ensure accuracy in its depiction of Polynesian culture and mythology.

- "The Social Network" (2010) used digital compositing to allow actor Armie Hammer to play both Winklevoss twins convincingly.

Music and Instruments

- The most expensive musical instrument ever sold is a Stradivarius violin, auctioned for $15.9 million.

- The didgeridoo, an indigenous Australian instrument, is believed to be one of the world's oldest wind instruments, dating back over 1,500 years.

- The "Mozart effect" suggests that listening to classical music may improve spatial reasoning skills, though its long-term impact is debated.

- Beethoven began to lose his hearing in his late 20s and composed some of his greatest works while nearly deaf.

- The theremin is a unique electronic instrument that is played without physical contact by moving hands near two metal antennas.

- The saxophone, now iconic in jazz, was originally invented as a classical instrument by Adolphe Sax.

- The human voice is capable of producing multiple tones simultaneously, a technique known as throat singing, used by Tuvan and Inuit cultures.

- The glass harmonica, designed by Benjamin Franklin, creates eerie tones by spinning glass bowls of different sizes.

- The piano has over 12,000 individual parts, and concert grand pianos require about a year to build.

- The world's largest pipe organ, with over 33,000 pipes, is housed in the Boardwalk Hall Auditorium in Atlantic City, New Jersey.

- A single violin is made from over 70 pieces of wood, carefully glued and fitted together.

- The shortest musical composition, "As Slow as Possible," is being performed in Germany and is set to last 639 years.

- The largest playable tuba requires two people to operate and stands over 7 feet tall.

- Some rock bands have included unusual instruments like typewriters, power drills, and vacuum cleaners in their performances.

- The world's longest concert by multiple artists lasted over 18 days and was held in Canada.

- The contrabassoon is the lowest-pitched woodwind instrument and is over 16 feet long.

- Playing an instrument uses nearly every region of the brain and can improve memory, coordination, and multitasking abilities.

- In Western classical music, the oboe often plays the "tuning note" for the orchestra, to which all other instruments tune.

- "The Four Seasons" by Vivaldi is considered one of the first examples of program music, evoking specific imagery for each season.

- Guitar strings were historically made from animal intestines, giving rise to the term "catgut," despite being more commonly sourced from sheep.

- Jazz musicians often use the term "woodshed" to refer to practicing in solitude, possibly originating from musicians practicing in outdoor sheds.

- The marimba, a type of xylophone from Africa and Latin America, has resonator tubes under its keys to enhance sound.

- Ocarinas, wind instruments often made of clay, are believed to have been played by ancient civilizations in the Americas and Asia.

- Inuit throat singing is traditionally performed as a friendly competition between two women to see who can outlast the other.

- The mbira, an African thumb piano, uses metal tines attached to a wooden board and often has bottle caps or shells attached for a buzzing sound.

- Ancient Greek amphitheaters were designed with advanced acoustics, allowing audiences of thousands to hear speakers on stage.

Imprint

MSDKI

195533 N 109th St, Scottsdale, AZ 85255, USA

ISBN: 9798345962282

First Edition
© 2024 Robert Brown